BECOMING BILITERATE
Young children learning different writing systems

Charmian Kenner

tb

Trentham Books

Stoke on Trent, UK and Sterling, USA

Trentham Books Limited

Westview House	22883 Quicksilver Drive
734 London Road	Sterling
Oakhill	VA 20166-2012
Stoke on Trent	USA
Staffordshire	
England ST4 5NP	

First published 2004
Reprinted 2006

British Library Cataloguing-in-Publication Data
A catalogue record for this book is available from the British Library

ISBN-13: 978-1-85856-319-0
ISBN-10: 1-85856-319-4

The author and publisher wish to thank the following for their kind permission to reproduce material: the parents of Selina, Ming, Tala, Yazan, Sadhana and Brian for the children's writing and drawing; Lambeth Chinese Community School and the UK Federation of Chinese Schools for Figures 7 and 11; the Arabic Community School in Hounslow for Figures 8, 14, 15, 32 and 36. It did not prove possible to contact the copyright owners for Figures 9, 17 and 18, although every effort was made to do so.

Cover pictures by Selina, aged six, with 'love' written in Chinese above the drawing of her mother and 'Girl Power' in Chinese above the drawing of her sister.

Designed and typeset by Trentham Print Design Ltd., Chester and printed in Great Britain by Bemrose Shafron (Printers) Ltd., Chester.

Contents

Acknowledgements

I would like to thank

Selina, Ming, Tala, Yazan, Sadhana and Brian: the children who showed us how they learned to write in Chinese, Arabic or Spanish at the same time as English

the children's families, for their hospitality and generous participation in the research project

the children's community language schools and primary schools, where teachers welcomed us and discussed the findings of the research: Lambeth Chinese Community School, the Arabic Community School in Hounslow, the Latin American Saturday School, and Berkeley, Duncombe, Eveline Lowe, Richard Atkins and Wellington Primary Schools

all the children who took part in the peer teaching sessions at primary school to learn Chinese, Arabic or Spanish

the Economic and Social Research Council, for funding the 'Signs of Difference' research project

Kate Rex and Sila Chawda, educators dedicated to supporting children's bilingual learning, for responding to the manuscript with comments and suggestions

Gillian Klein, for her editing skills and her personal involvement with the message of the book

John Stipling and Shawn Stipling for their excellent work on design and typesetting

and finally, the research team: Gunther Kress, Hayat Al-Khatib, Gwen Kwok, Roy Kam and Kuan-Chun Tsai – our joint thinking shaped the ideas in this book

Para mi hijo Darío
Verte crecer bilingüe ha sido una alegría

For my son Darío
It has been a pleasure to see you grow up bilingual

Introduction

'Who would like to write on the board?'

Several children's hands go up, and the teacher picks out five-year-old Tala. She comes confidently to the board and writes the word for 'rabbit' in Arabic (arnab). Her writing is clear, going from right to left, showing the detail of each letter and its join to the following one, since – as Tala's eight-year-old brother Khalid explains to me later – 'all Arabic writing is joined-up'. The teacher praises Tala and she goes proudly back to her seat.

Watching Tala in her class at community language school, I realise that my research on early biliteracy has begun. I have just witnessed a five-year-old demonstrate her capabilities as a bilingual writer – for Tala is also learning English at primary school, where she writes entries in her journal each Monday morning telling of weekend escapades with her siblings and cousins. Sometimes Tala's emergent writing refers to her Arabic school as part of her weekend activities: 'I went to a party at my Arabic school. It was really fun...The next day me my brother and my sister and my parents had a barbecue at my cousin's house'.

Tala's Arabic school takes place on Saturday mornings in West London and is run by dedicated volunteers. Her teacher Enas brings in fluffy toy animals for the children so that they can match each toy with the animal's name written in Arabic. She also creates home-made visual aids by gluing pictures onto the back of cereal packets. She looks for dual-language books at the local library, and reads the well-known English story *Where's Spot?* to the class with great expression in Arabic.

At Tala's primary school, she shows her friends how to write in Arabic, reminding them to start from the right-hand side of the page not the left ('We don't start from there, we start from here!') and checking their efforts in detail ('You forgot to do that little wiggly line'). As her primary school teacher sees Tala's interest in Arabic script and her understanding of how it works, she is impressed by the abilities of young children to learn languages early.

With the encouragement of her teachers and her family, Tala has the chance to become literate in Arabic as well as English. She will be able to enjoy stories, books and newspapers which open windows into different cultural worlds. Her opportunities for work and study will be widened considerably. At a time when early language learning is being promoted in England and other countries, Tala and her Arabic school classmates are leading the way.

This book tells the story of six children learning to write in Chinese, Arabic or Spanish as well as English. I follow the children's progress over the period of one year, as each turns six years old. Selina, Ming, Tala, Yazan, Sadhana and Brian can explore two writing systems at the same time. They can also teach their primary school classmates about writing in another language. Their pupils respond eagerly, fascinated by different scripts and the meanings that can be made through them.

Teachers and parents sometimes think that young children will be confused if they are dealing with more than one writing system. However, children have many more capabilities than we realise. They are constantly investigating the written world around them, finding out what graphic symbols stand for and how they can be used to communicate with others.

The early years – when children are at their most flexible in mind and body – are an excellent time to learn about different writing systems and try out different scripts. This book will provide reassurance and guidance for educators who teach young bilinguals, and those who are keen to offer multilingual literacy experience in the primary school classroom. Each chapter ends with practical suggestions for teachers, to expand your own understanding and address issues around biliteracy in your classroom.

The book is organised as follows:

Chapter One: Learning at home, community school and primary school

Biliteracy evolves through a combination of different learning experiences, as children encounter the ideas offered by parents, siblings, other family members and teachers. This chapter sets the scene by introducing Brian, Sadhana, Yazan, Tala, Ming and Selina and describing their learning contexts.

Chapter Two: Understanding different writing systems

At the age of five or six, children are already capable of understanding that writing systems work in different ways. Selina and Ming understand that Chinese is not alphabetic, but based on characters which represent words. Tala and Yazan know that Arabic letters change form when written at the beginning, in the middle or at the end of a word. Sadhana and Brian are aware that Spanish and English have a similar alphabet but with some different letter-sound relationships. We see how children's ideas build up over time, and how biliterate experience stimulates their thinking.

Chapter Three: Writing different scripts

As well as investigating how writing systems work, children are concerned with the act of writing itself – how symbols look and how to create them. Each script helps the learner to develop different capacities as a writer. In Chinese, children need to remember complex visual patterns and distinguish between strokes of slightly different length and angle. In Arabic, children write in a different direction from English and look out for the dots that differentiate otherwise identical letters. In Spanish, children learn to write accents above letters and find out that n and ñ represent different sounds. Through biliteracy, children can build up a range of visual and actional abilities – multisemiotic resources, which are an advantage in today's world of multimodal communication.

Chapter Four: Living in simultaneous worlds

Children look for connections between their learning experiences, making sense of their lives as a whole. Yazan and Tala can draw on Arabic or English or both, when speaking and writing. Brian and Sadhana live their daily lives in Spanish and English. Ming and Selina are growing up as British Chinese. These children live in simultaneous worlds rather than two separate worlds. This chapter shows how they make use of the links as well as the differences between their writing systems, giving them alternative ways to construct their knowledge and identities.

Chapter Five: Literacy teaching systems in bilingual families

In a bilingual family, the literacy knowledge of different members (parents, siblings, grandparents, aunts and uncles) is harnessed to complement each other in supporting children's learning. The patterns of interdependence within the families of Selina, Ming, Tala, Yazan, Sadhana and Brian can be seen as literacy eco-systems. Each family has its own way of helping children to become biliterate in Chinese, Arabic or Spanish as well as English. This makes us aware of the potential variety of systems used by families, so that as educators we will be better placed to offer further support for children's learning.

In the conclusion, I sum up the benefits of early language learning and argue that as many children as possible should have the opportunity to speak and write in different languages. In moving towards a multilingual society, our aims need to be two-fold: to expand the knowledge which bilingual children already possess, and to offer language learning possibilities to monolingual children. In this way, we will help children to become accomplished communicators who can draw on a range of different cultural experiences. These young people will grow up well equipped to benefit from and contribute to our complex global community.

1

Learning at home, community school and primary school

School is just one of the places where children learn. Home is another equally vital place, together with the community in which each child grows up. Some children's lives include more than one school. When I first visited Brian and enquired how he was getting on at school, he asked which one I meant: English school or 'español escuela?' (his name for Spanish school).

Home, school and community together make up the pieces in the jigsaw of children's lives. Children are constantly uniting the pieces in their learning, but how far do we recognise this? When I visited Selina, Ming, Sadhana, Brian, Tala and Yazan and their families, each visit revealed more of the richness and complexity of the children's home learning. I could see how children were bringing together their experiences from primary school, Saturday school, and the wider world – and re-working these experiences with the help of siblings, parents and other family members.

Many scenes come to mind: Tala and her brother making greetings cards together, Sadhana and her mother poring over a large Spanish-English dictionary, Ming writing on the computer with his brother's help, Yazan doing spelling tests in English and Arabic with his sister, Selina and her sister creating their own pop magazines, Brian and his brother showing me the board game they had made with their father. In this chapter I begin to build up a picture of each child's contexts for learning, looking at the input offered to them by their families and community school teachers in addition to their experiences at primary school.

Finding out about home and community learning

To discover how children learn outside school, we need to observe with an open mind, over time and in detail. Researchers have started to work in this way, visiting families at home and attending community events. By watching what takes place, the researcher builds up an understanding of children's learning experiences. Interviews with parents, children and other family members can also explain how and why these activities happen.

The in-depth picture built up by researchers is available as a resource for classroom educators. Although teachers cannot be continually present in every home and community, they can gain insights into the events and issues that may be significant in children's lives. Teachers can then use these ideas as a springboard to find out more about the children they work with.

Our eyes were first opened to the variety of children's learning outside school by Shirley Brice Heath's long-term ethnographic observation of language and literacy use in rural communities in the United States (1983), followed by work such as that of Denny Taylor and Cathe Dorsey-Gaines (1988) with families living in poverty in New York City. These studies showed that all families offered learning experiences to young children, which differed depending on the communities' contexts and values.

Researchers began to look at a range of families from different cultural backgrounds, including many who were bilingual or multilingual. In studies carried out in Britain and other English-dominant countries, it has become clear that children's learning in languages other than English is important. Not only can children speak different languages, they are often attending classes to read and write as well. They can combine their knowledge from all these sources to enrich their overall learning.

Bilingual learning happens from a very early age. Rose Drury (Parke *et al*, 2002) made a case study of four-year-old Samia from Watford, north of London. Drury discovered that at home she engaged in roleplay with her two-year-old brother Sadaqat, based on her experiences at nursery school. As the 'teacher', Samia explained to Sadaqat how to paint a picture in different colours, using the instructions she had heard in English from her nursery teacher and switching into their home language, Pahari, when he needed clarification. This discovery was only made by listening to recordings from a radio-microphone worn by Samia. Her nursery teacher thought that Samia did not yet speak any English and had no idea she could operate simultaneously in English and Pahari.

My own research in a multilingual nursery class in South London (Kenner, 2000) demonstrated that three- and four-year-olds pay attention to the written languages used in their environment as well as to spoken languages. When families were asked to bring literacy materials such as calendars and videos from home to school, and parents were invited to write in their own languages in the classroom, children commented on the different scripts and used them to make their own texts. Meera's posters about her favourite Bollywood video, Recep's Turkish newspaper, and Mohammed's Arabic alphabet chart all stemmed from materials that were part of daily life at home.

Community events give varied opportunities for children to learn. When Dinah Volk and Martha de Acosta (2001) observed Puerto Rican five-year-olds growing up in a midwestern US city, they noted the importance of church-based activities for literacy development. Through participating in church services, children gained knowledge of the words and phrases used, which was then further explored as they read the Bible aloud in Spanish with a parent, or incorporated their own version of prayers into play with siblings. In many home literacy events, particularly with siblings, Spanish and English were both used to mediate children's understanding.

The special contribution of community schools
Some parents teach their children to read and write in different literacies at home, as An (2000) describes in her research about Chinese families in Britain. However, many families find the support of community language schools vital. From the age of five or six onwards children begin to attend community schools for literacy learning, often along with other cultural activities such as music, art and dance. These voluntary organisations are now being termed 'complementary schools', in recognition of the role they play in supporting and extending children's mainstream learning.

Eve Gregory, Nasima Rashid and Ann Williams found that six-year-old children of Bangladeshi origin in East London study both Bengali and Arabic at community language school. The researchers observed the learning taking place in these community classes and also asked children to tape-record activities which they commonly did at home. The recordings revealed that older siblings used methods from community school as well as those from English primary school to support younger children's literacy development at home (Rashid and Gregory, 1997; Gregory and Williams, 2000).

Each kind of community class has a different part to play in children's learning. In the Gujarati and Urdu-speaking Muslim community in north-east London studied by Raymonde Sneddon (2000), children could use the cultural and leisure facilities of the local Gujarati community centre, and also attended classes to become literate in Urdu for religious purposes. At the age of seven, the children were creative storytellers in both Gujarati and English, and were accustomed to discussing complex questions on text comprehension in their Urdu classes. This discussion took place in English and Gujarati as well as Urdu, and Sneddon suggests that if children are adept at negotiating meanings between three languages, they can use similar strategies when reading in the English mainstream classroom.

Children are aware of the opportunities available to them in each site of learning. The five-year-olds interviewed by Leena Helavaara Robertson (2002) attended Arabic and Urdu classes as well as their primary school in Watford, England. They explained that Arabic was useful for reading the Qur'an, Urdu for communicating with their families and English for school work. They were keen to learn all these literacies, each for an important purpose in their lives. Drawing on their experience from three classrooms, the children were already able to translate words and to examine how they were written in each script. They compared sound systems in different languages, pointing out for example that English has only one 'd' sound while Urdu has two. This metalinguistic awareness stands children in good stead throughout their language development.

Keeping in mind this wide range of experiences contributing to young bilingual children's learning, let us turn to the particular worlds of the six children in this book. For the research project, we first made contact with their families at community language school and then visited each child at home.

Selina and Ming: growing up with Chinese and English

Selina and Ming attended the same primary school in South London, and the same voluntary-run Chinese school on Saturday mornings. Both families had lived in Britain for at least twenty years, since arriving from Hong Kong. The children lived with their parents and siblings in flats in two different blocks, around the corner from their primary school. Selina had an older sister aged ten and a brother aged fourteen and Ming had five older brothers and sisters ranging in age from twelve to 24.

Selina's home

On our first visit to Selina's family, we arrived at their third-floor flat at six o'clock in the evening and found a Chinese lesson in full progress. Seated round the kitchen table, Selina and her sister Susannah were working hard on separate tasks, supervised by their mother. We later discovered that this lesson took place every evening for at least an hour, to supplement the children's community language classes.

Selina was practising the Chinese characters she was currently learning at Saturday school, writing each one with meticulous care. She was using a pencil so that she could rub out any mistakes noticed by her mother. Meanwhile, ten-year-old Susannah was reading out a long passage from her Chinese school textbook. To remind herself of the sounds of some of the characters, she was noting them down in Roman script. Her mother was on hand to support her.

Both girls were absorbed in the lesson, with Selina being keen to produce well-written characters for her own satisfaction as well as her mother's, although they sometimes argued about the details. Later Selina showed how she could read out a passage in Cantonese, and then in Mandarin (Chinese writing is the same for both spoken languages). Susannah was finding out how to use a Chinese dictionary, which is organised according to particular stroke patterns, not alphabetically as English would be.

The living-room walls in Selina's home showed how family life included aspects of both Chinese and English culture. Alongside a photo of her parents' wedding and red banners with gold writing for Chinese New Year, there was a poster depicting Selina's favourite English pop group, S Club 7. Music and songs in English and Chinese were part of Selina's repertoire. Her mother and sister entered into her enthusiasm; when

Selina showed us lyrics by S Club 7 in the magazine *Song Words*, she pointed out 'Mummy's song' and 'my sister's song'. With Christmas coming up, Selina gave us a spirited rendition of the carol Silent Night in English, using the words written out from primary school as a back-up, and followed it with Jingle Bells. She also demonstrated her prowess in singing songs in Mandarin, taught by her mother, including a version of Happy Birthday to You.

The television provided another varied source of culture. The family subscribed to TV stations from Taiwan and Hong Kong, and Selina and her siblings would watch a Chinese serial and then switch to Who Wants to be a Millionaire? in English. Selina knew the times of the Chinese serials and could identify the star actors in the Chinese TV guides. Literacy and spoken language were thus developing for Selina via her immersion in popular culture in both English and Chinese. Such material is highly motivating for children and contributes to their learning, as shown by recent research on uses of popular culture in homes around the world (Marsh, forthcoming).

Literacy based around English school was also part of Selina's home life. She kept her schoolwork tidily in a child-size desk in the living-room, with a collection of storybooks and non-fiction books – such as a big book on *Questions and Answers* – in a small bookcase nearby. With Susannah, she played language games they knew from school, such as

Figure 1: Selina's writing of a Chinese New Year message, given a mark of 100% by her older sister Susannah.

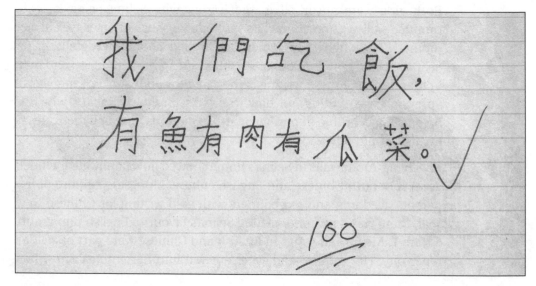

guessing words in Hangman or making a finger flap game where each flap opened to reveal a different word.

Susannah played and worked with Selina in a host of activities in English and Chinese. The sisters made greetings cards together in English, and cards in Chinese for Chinese New Year. They created magazines about S Club 7 with pictures of the pop group members, little booklets on topics such as 'Things I like', bookmarks decorated with hearts, and colourful pictures of butterflies. Susannah helped her sister with English homework, and prepared her for next Saturday's Chinese lesson by practising the characters that would be involved. Figure 1 shows how Susannah, as teacher, gave Selina a mark of 100% for her writing of a Chinese New Year message.

Ming's home

Ming, like Selina, used two Chinese languages at home as well as English. Whilst Selina's mother spoke both Mandarin and Cantonese, Ming's family spoke mainly Hakka, another Chinese language. His mother also spoke Cantonese and Ming understood some of this. His family possessed a Chinese-English dictionary and Ming knew its purpose: once when I visited with an advisor to the research project who knew Mandarin but not Hakka or Cantonese, Ming fetched the dictionary and presented it to us to help with our linguistic dilemma!

Ming noticed the use of Chinese writing in everyday life, asking 'why Chinese?' when looking at the calendar on the living-room wall of his family's flat, and commenting on the characters he saw when visiting a large Chinese supermarket in South London. In the shop, he would look for his favourite foods on the shelves, such as prawn crackers and jelly.

Ming's older siblings, particularly his twelve-year-old brother, helped him with his homework from Chinese Saturday school. On Thursday or Friday evenings Ming practised writing the characters. He knew his brother could translate and would ask him the meaning of Chinese words in English. Another activity they did together was based around Japanese cartoon stories, copying pictures from magazines or computer games and adding some words in Chinese. To show us his knowledge of Chinese characters, Ming made a chart where he could practise some of the characters he had learnt – with the addition of a symbol used in both Chinese and English, an arrow (Figure 2).

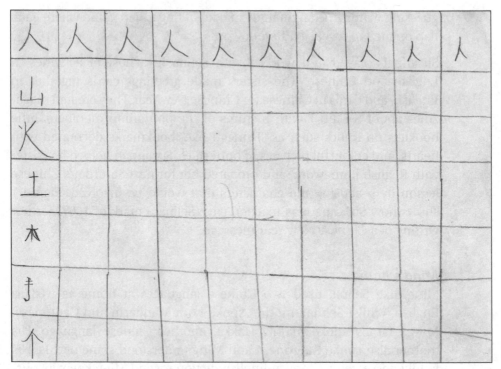

Figure 2: Chart made by Ming to practise Chinese characters.

His siblings were also a resource for Ming's learning of English literacy. He read storybooks brought from primary school to his brother and sisters, asking for help when he needed it. We watched Ming sitting on the sofa, being helped informally by his sisters to carry out his plan of drawing a 'spider house' in a new notebook we had presented to him, and asking them how to write his older brother's name. They also helped him to write greetings cards, providing him with a model so that he could write 'Merry Christmas' and add his name.

On the shelves in the living-room were a number of non-fiction books in English for the family's use, and Ming also saw his older brothers and sisters referring to texts for their courses at secondary school and college. Each helped their younger siblings with school and college work, sitting together on the sofa to consult the books concerned. Ming witnessed these discussions taking place, and would ask his siblings what they were doing. Although there was little space to store items in the flat, a substantial file of Ming's own primary school work had been kept from the previous year, which he proudly showed me.

Audiovisual texts relating to popular culture were Ming's preferred form of entertainment and learning. He enjoyed cartoons from Hong Kong in Cantonese, and computer games in English were a favourite activity. His older brother allowed Ming to play on his computer every day after school, provided he had finished his schoolwork. There were two computers in the living-room, one on either side of the TV screen. Whilst other family members watched TV, Ming and his twelve-year-old brother each used one computer, or played together so that Ming could receive help with drawing and writing. When showing his collection of computer games, Ming could identify the different boxes and give the name of each game.

Ming also loved his collection of Pokémon magazines and cards and could read out the numbers quantifying the magic forces that belonged to each Pokémon character. Catalogues were another source of fascination and he would turn the pages, asking for toys that he wanted.

Tala and Yazan: Arabic-English bilinguals

Tala and Yazan both lived with their parents and siblings in West London housing estates close to Heathrow Airport. Planes descended constantly over Yazan's primary school, with Tala's close by. On Saturday mornings, the two children attended the same Arabic community school. Tala's family was Palestinian and she was born just after they arrived in Britain. Yazan's family had come from Syria two years ago. Both children were the youngest in their families. Tala's brother was eight years old and her sister eleven. Yazan's sister was ten.

Tala's home

Encouraged by her family, Tala was a keen performer in Arabic. When we visited, she recited the alphabet for us and sang songs, including one in standard Arabic with many verses about 'my country' and another in Egyptian dialect which she had learnt from satellite TV. She had won a prize for volunteering to tell the story of Ibrahim from the Qur'an at her Saturday school, and could recite verses from the Qur'an too. The family's study of the Qur'an was supported by a CD-ROM which brought the entire text to the computer screen. The recitation of each section could be heard in Arabic, and clicking on any line revealed a written English translation.

Tala's mother taught at the Saturday school and helped her children with their Arabic homework on Friday evenings. Tala also saw Arabic being written in letters to family and asked her mother what the writing said. In addition, the family had access to nine channels of Arabic television, from countries ranging from Tunisia to Qatar. The TV was often tuned to the news channel, and Tala could recognise the words meaning 'breaking news' and would call the rest of the family to come. She knew the times of her favourite Syrian and Egyptian soap operas and followed the lives of the characters.

English TV was popular with the three siblings for children's programmes such as Blue Peter, cartoons, and comedy shows, including Mr. Bean. Tala would read programme titles such as Rug Rats off the screen. The children watched these programmes on their own television in one of their bedrooms, or in the living room where either parents or children would switch channels according to interest.

Tala's enjoyment of performance was also evident in English. She recited the alphabet and counted to a hundred. She sang nursery rhymes to us: Twinkle Twinkle Little Star, Old McDonald had a Farm, and an updated playground version of Humpty Dumpty. She could invent her own rhyming songs in English, helped by practising rhymes with her sister. When Nagam started with 'cat', Tala responded with many words which rhymed. When Nagam presented her with a greater challenge, 'lemon', Tala rose to the occasion by suggesting 'come on'.

Figure 3: Tala writing words at home in Arabic and English.

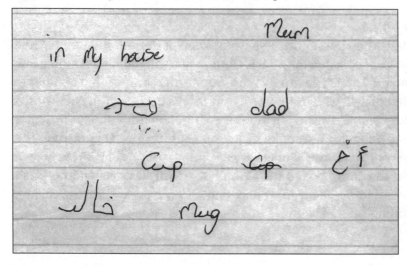

English literacy was involved in many of the activities Tala did with her parents and siblings. When her mother wrote a shopping list in Arabic, Tala would make her own version in English. Seeing her mother practising the written part of the driving test, she ticked the boxes for the answers, and she tried to help her sister with a grammar test. The three children made greetings cards together, with Tala asking Nagam or her brother Khalid for help with some of the words. She liked to read storybooks from primary school to herself or to her mother, who remarked that Tala needed little assistance. Figure 3 shows a piece of writing by Tala at home in which she was trying out both Arabic and English.

Yazan's home

When we first visited Yazan's house, he was shy but intrigued, peering down at us from the top of the stairs. Eventually he 'posted' an envelope to us through the banisters, enclosing two sheets of paper on which he had written his name in English together with arrows, a heart, and stars. When his favourite programme from Syria came on TV, he could no longer resist venturing down the stairs towards the living-room.

His connections with Syria were important to Yazan. Together with his sister Lana, he showed me photo albums of the summer holidays the family continued to spend there and talked about his relatives and the places they had visited. His mother told me of a letter Yazan had written to his grandmother, saying 'Nanny I love you, I want to come to Syria'. He had asked his mother for help, and wanted to write in both Arabic and English.

Arabic was the language mostly used at home, and Yazan was happy with this situation. When his sister used English he would remind her 'Don't speak English at home, at home Arabic'. He preferred his mother to use Arabic when writing shopping lists, dictating items to her and even insisting that she wrote 'cornflakes' in Arabic. However, he was also interested in the relationship between Arabic and English, and constantly asked for translations of what he heard or saw at home or on the street, showing surprise when he discovered a word such as 'bus' was the same in both languages.

When he came home from Saturday school, Yazan often wanted to do his Arabic homework straight away. He would ask his mother 'Can you watch me – if I'm correct or not correct?' She would keep an eye on him and comment as appropriate, putting dots on the page so that he could

Figure 4: Lana helping Yazan to work with numbers in Arabic and English.

trace the outline of difficult letters. Lana also taught Yazan how to write, in both Arabic and English, using exercise books and a small white-board in her bedroom to demonstrate examples.

Yazan's learning was enriched by books and films as well as television. Lana read her brother bedtime stories in Arabic and English and gave explanations in answer to his questions. As well as English videos, the children had films dubbed into Arabic which they could watch on their computer. While they watched *A Bug's Life*, they translated key phrases into English for my benefit. Games were also an opportunity for learning. Yazan and Lana played educational computer games about language and mathematics together, in English, and had several board games such as Snakes and Ladders.

Yazan's bedroom contained a variety of materials that stimulated language and literacy development. He had a cassette player with tapes in both English and Arabic, and a small blackboard on the wall of his room on which, he told me, he did something different every day. He rubbed out the hearts he had drawn in chalk to replace them with my name, his own and Lana's in English. His little desk, decorated with Bart Simpson stickers in Arabic and other stickers in English, was crammed with papers, including Arabic and English work he had done with Lana (see Figure 4 for examples). On his chair was a collection of English magazines and newspapers, including a computer magazine and a toy catalogue in which he pointed out the toys he would like to get, reading out the prices as '75' for £2.75 and '99' for £20.99.

Sadhana and Brian: Latino Londoners

Sadhana and Brian attended the same Latin American Saturday school in southwest London, to learn to read and write in Spanish. But each lived in another part of the city. Like many parents, theirs were prepared to travel far to take their children to a particular school they had heard about from friends. Sadhana lived with her mother in an eighth-floor flat in a high-rise block in southeast London. Brian and his parents, grandmother and eight-year-old brother lived in a terraced house in North London, part of a housing co-operative originally set up by the local Latin American community. Both children had only a short walk to their local primary school. The families had come to England – Sadhana's from Ecuador and Brian's from Colombia – shortly before the children were born.

Sadhana's home

Sadhana was an only child whose home was full of social interaction. Aunts and uncles shared the flat or were daily visitors, and Sadhana often spent time with her cousin Vanessa, also six years old, who lived nearby. Sadhana's grandmother visited from Ecuador at least once a year and her mother went to Ecuador once or twice a year, taking Sadhana with her when she could. In between these trips, Sadhana spoke to her grandmother regularly on the phone in Spanish.

As with all the children in the research project, Sadhana's home was a place where more than one language was used. Her mother was accustomed to speaking English and her aunts and uncles were learning it, so although Spanish was the main language of communication, there was a good deal of switching between languages. Sadhana saw herself as helping one of her aunts, who was currently attending classes, to learn English. The family had a large Spanish-English dictionary to which they referred when reading and writing in English, to check spelling and understanding.

Sadhana's mother supported her daughter's learning of Spanish and English literacy whenever she asked for help. Sadhana liked to do her Saturday school homework in Spanish by herself if it was easy, and would ask about words she did not know, such as *culebra* (snake). She read storybooks from primary school with her mother, giving her own version when she had heard her mother's. When reading in English, she would look for words beginning with the same letter, for example all the 'S' words like 'snake', or 'M' words from 'mum' to 'Monday'.

To aid Sadhana's primary school learning, her mother bought her a substantial book called *My World* containing information and colourful visuals about many of the topics dealt with at school, such as 'How plants grow' or 'Festivals'. Sadhana turned the pages of this book, making comments in English such as 'This is the seed that is grown ... there's lots of worms in the soil' and describing in detail how to make a pumpkin lantern for Hallowe'en, because seeing the picture and instructions in the book reminded her that she had done this activity at Spanish school.

Many of Sadhana's everyday literacy experiences were in English, such as looking through catalogues with her mother to choose items, and trying to fill in the form. When walking along the street she would spell out words from street signs, for example P-I-Z-Z-A, and insist on

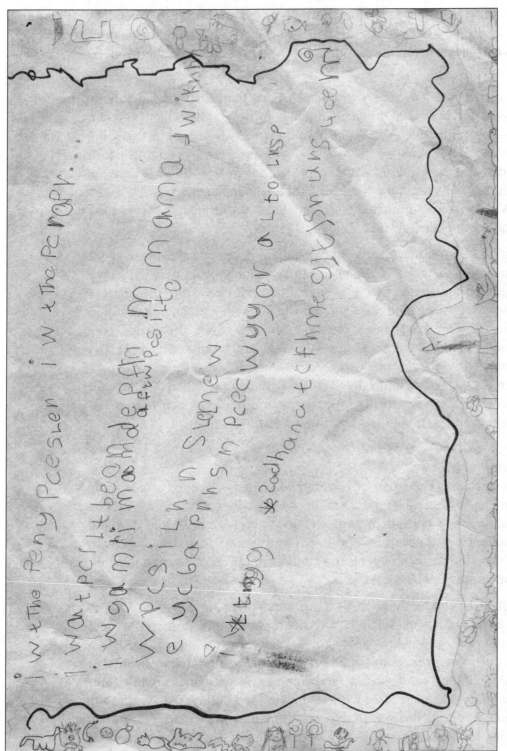

Figure 5: Sadhana's story 'I went to the park': 'mama' (mum) appears in the second and third line and 'Sadhana' in the last line.

knowing what they stood for. She also saw her mother writing greetings cards in Spanish or English, and made her own cards including pictures of herself and her mother, putting her mother's name, 'Elizabeth', on the envelope.

Sadhana had less access to Spanish texts than English ones, partly because her mother found it difficult to obtain children's books in Spanish, and cable TV in Spanish was too expensive. Sadhana had some videos of cartoons in Spanish, and she was fond of certain English videos, such as *Splash*, which captured her imagination because the central character in the film was a mermaid and Sadhana loved water. TV and videos stimulated Sadhana's literacy learning; she would ask about words she saw on the screen.

In play and in her own writing, Sadhana developed her ideas about literacy. With her cousin Vanessa, she saw an opportunity to write on a steamed-up window in the kitchen, and both girls wrote their names there. Sadhana would draw and write in her bedroom; on one occasion she asked for pencil and paper when she was in bed, and produced a long text which she read back as 'I went to the park' (Figure 5). The emergent writing is mainly based on English, with the word 'mama' appearing twice ('mum' in Spanish is 'mamá'). Sadhana's talent for drawing is evident in the intricate picture border which frames her writing and is an important part of the text.

Brian's home

Brian and his eight-year-old brother Julian had a resource which is rare for children growing up in London: a street where they could play. The cul-de-sac in which their terraced house stood was quiet and safe, and the two boys hurtled up and down on bikes or played football with friends from adjoining houses. Families could keep an eye on the children from their balconies.

Often the children were to be found indoors, doing things together at the table in the open-plan kitchen/living-room, including reading and homework, or watching television. Several activities might be going on at once. On my second visit, Brian and Julian were watching a video of the children's story *Aladdin* and jumping in excitement, whilst also coming to the table to do writing, drawing and cutting out. Next to the table was a sideboard with drawers containing the children's Saturday school work from the current and previous year, as well as other texts they had made such as stories written in old diaries. A mug full of pens for the children's use stood on the sideboard.

Brian's mother told how Brian always wanted to participate whenever someone was writing in the household. He insisted on adding his name and the date to birthday and Christmas cards being sent to Colombia. He liked to write his brother's name as well as his own; the boys were very close, almost like twins. They wrote and made things together,

Figure 6: Brian's picture of the cowboy cartoon character 'El Nombre'.

using straws to make models of skeletons or playing the word and number games in the BBC magazine *Learning is Fun*, brought home from school and kept in the sideboard drawer. They had also made a game with their father, a board game with a numbered track along which you could advance by throwing a dice. Brian and Julian explained the rules to me.

Brian was keen on schoolwork and often wanted to do his homework from Spanish or English school as soon as he came home, even if his mother was preparing tea and could not help right away. Julian supported his brother's reading in English, listening to him read short easy books brought from primary school. The children's grandmother lived with them and she was able to help with work in Spanish.

The family's main resource for Spanish literacy learning, apart from materials brought home from Saturday school, consisted of two beginner books for children from Colombia. Brian and Julian used these with their mother, as support for the work they did at Spanish school. On video, they owned *El Rey León* (The Lion King), but most of their videos were in English, such as *Aladdin*, apart from some Spanish films rented from a video shop in South London. The family did not yet have cable or satellite TV in Spanish. Brian and Julian enjoyed the appearance of a cowboy character with a Spanish name, *El Nombre*, in a cartoon on English TV, and drew him in the notebooks they kept in the sideboard drawer (see Figure 6).

Brian's family, like all the families in the research project, had much easier access to English than their home language. They were surrounded by English from primary school, television and the wider world. Nevertheless Brian's parents and grandmother wished him to become literate in Spanish as well as English, and the families of Sadhana, Ming, Selina, Yazan and Tala had the same desire for their children. We look now at the reasons for their decisions, and the important role of the children's community language schools in helping them on the path to biliteracy.

Advantages of bilingualism and biliteracy

Each family had more than one reason for deciding to send their children to Saturday school. An important motive for everyone was to keep up links with the extended family, and to help children feel part of their wider linguistic and cultural community. Parents also recognised that growing up bilingual and biliterate would be an advantage to their children, enhancing communication and job opportunities in a multilingual world.

Selina's mother expressed her desire for Selina to stay connected with her Chinese heritage: 'If she doesn't speak Chinese, I feel disappointed'. She also raised the issue of Selina's sense of identity, pointing out that 'she looks Chinese, so people will expect her to speak it'. Chinese would add to Selina's range of skills and enable her to contribute to society: 'When she grows up she can help people'. Selina's mother believed that the best time for children to learn Chinese was when very young, because they had a greater facility for pronunciation and it was easier to learn to write the characters.

Ming's mother linked knowledge of the Chinese writing system with cultural identity. She wanted her children to learn how to read and write Chinese characters 'because we are Chinese'. If they visited Hong Kong or China, they would be able to speak with relatives, and they could use basic reading and writing to orient themselves in that society. Ming's older brother, for example, was able to fill in the landing card in Chinese on the plane to Hong Kong.

Tala's mother said that the family had two reasons for wanting Tala to attend Saturday school. First was the need to learn the language: 'her mother language is Arabic' and she had 'to be able to understand what is her background'. Secondly came 'her culture': the knowledge she would gain by mixing with children from similar backgrounds. Tala's mother highlighted the connection between language and culture: 'if she is Arab she will be expected to know Arabic, otherwise she'll be laughed at'.

Yazan's family also saw Arabic as his mother tongue, and wanted him to retain it, both for keeping up contact with relatives and because they might return to Syria in the future. Yazan's parents also emphasised the benefits of bilingualism and multilingualism, stating that it is good for children to grow up with two or three languages.

Sadhana's mother made a similar point about how bilingualism could widen opportunities for her daughter in the future. Knowing both Spanish and English would help Sadhana in her professional life as well as facilitating family links: being bilingual meant being able to participate in *comunicación* in the widest sense.

For Brian's parents and his grandmother, Brian's attendance at Saturday school was important in order to maintain his Spanish, so that communication was easier within the family and within the local community; several of their neighbours in the housing co-operative were Latin American. Knowledge of Spanish would also make it possible for Brian to participate in everyday life when visiting Colombia. The family had observed Latin American children in London losing their Spanish, and had heard about the problems that arose when children felt left out during visits to Colombia.

Brian's mother was also aware of the importance of Spanish as a world language, and of the advantages of bilingualism. She herself had planned to become a bilingual secretary in Colombia, and now wanted to study French and Italian. She encouraged her children to learn other languages whenever possible. For example, Brian's brother Julian had attended a French club at primary school.

Parents' understanding of these issues is well supported by research evidence. Children who maintain their mother tongue as well as learning English feel connected to their families and communities (Mills, 2001). They can develop flexible multilingual identities linking different aspects of their lives, thus enabling them to feel part of a multicultural society (Martin *et al*, 2004). Bilingualism and biliteracy are important skills which increase communicative ability and open doors, ranging from study abroad to international business, to work with different ethnic communities. These skills are sadly lacking amongst the general population in Britain, a problem highlighted by the Nuffield Languages Inquiry (2000). The Inquiry underlined the need to promote multilingualism in order to gain all the benefits mentioned above.

Children attending community language school have a head start in language learning. Despite the difficult circumstances in which many such schools operate – being voluntary-run and having to make ends meet – teachers work with determination and dedication to help their pupils grow up bilingual and biliterate.

Learning at Chinese school
At the Cantonese-speaking Saturday school attended by Ming and Selina, between two and three hundred pupils studied in a dozen or more classes at different levels. The school had its own exercise books, the front cover of which is shown in Figure 7. Rules were printed on the

林拔芙華人社區學校

Lambeth Chinese Community School

姓名： 黎 錫 明

班別： _____

科目： _____

Figure 7: Front cover of the Chinese Saturday school exercise book.

back cover concerning work and behaviour. As well as literacy instruction, children could benefit from classes in dance and music. The school was linked with a local Chinese community centre which offered activity sessions in school holidays, such as crafts and Chinese chess. The annual Chinese New Year celebration enabled children to show their skills in front of an audience of families and the wider community, including the local Mayor, and Selina was a keen participant in the dance displays.

Ming, Selina and their classmates learned to write Chinese characters in their exercise books, paying careful attention to detail. This process is described more fully in Chapter Three. On our first visit to the school, I was struck by children's concentration as they practised the characters, each child involved in their work, some resting their heads on their arms as they wrote. In one class, children worked for half an hour in this way, in near silence. The teacher would circulate to offer help and advice, and children also compared the characters they had written with their friends' writing, leading to discussion about who was right or wrong. They were eager to show that they knew more complex characters, which were harder to write.

Textbooks with pictures of objects and everyday scenes provided support for learning. Children began to read short descriptions about topics such as Birthdays and An Autumn Day, building up to longer and more complicated texts. Games, such as team competitions to write characters on the board, and stories read by the teacher also formed part of the lessons. Ming's teacher, Debbie, told the story of a big fish who bullied a smaller fish but was caught in a net by fishermen, and discussed with the class the moral involved: 'You might be big and strong but you shouldn't look down on other people'.

Pupils at the school ranged from five-year-olds to teenagers. A four-year-old had also joined Ming's class, and she proved to be a thoughtful language learner, coming to the board to point out a particular detail when the teacher was writing a Chinese character. At the school's annual prizegiving assembly, children of all ages received prizes for doing well in tests and for working hard and being helpful in class. The teenagers were in evidence, helping to organise the event and participating in a short play, chatting and laughing together and taking pictures. A number of them had been successful in the GCSE exam for Chinese, a nationally-recognised qualification.

Learning at Arabic school

The Arabic community school had around two hundred pupils, whose families came from all parts of the Arab world, ranging from Lebanon to Somalia. The teachers were also from different countries and spoke different dialects of Arabic, whilst teaching the children to write in Modern Standard Arabic. The school held an annual Arabic Festival at which parents ran stalls with crafts and food from each country, while children held a 'fashion parade' of clothes from different countries and performed songs, poetry and dances. Yazan and Tala joined in with these activities, with Tala helping to lead some of the songs. Tala's mother – who was one of the teachers – developed a play in Arabic with the older pupils.

The school's headteacher held meetings with parents to discuss the curriculum, at which lively debates took place. Textbooks were based on a curriculum from Jordan, but the school recognised that British Arab children were studying in a different context and considered ways of adapting the material. Two of the teachers, including Tala's mother, undertook a secondary school teaching qualification in Arabic and a European language. From their training, they were able to share knowledge of mainstream school teaching methods with their colleagues.

With the help of picture cards, toys and jigsaws, Tala and Yazan and the other children in the youngest class studied the alphabet and learned to match words with the items they represented. They practised their writing of letters and words in photocopied booklets made by the school, with pictures to colour. They then progressed to colourful textbooks showing scenes from life in an Arab country, focusing on a particular family. Children gradually learned to read the accompanying text and do the associated grammatical exercises, and to understand the cartoon stories in the books. Numeracy was also part of the classes: the youngest children were practising addition and subtraction, using numerals written in Arabic.

The school had a GCSE and an A-level class for Arabic, thus offering qualifications at the same level as those obtainable at secondary school. However, children often took these exams earlier than the usual ages of sixteen and eighteen. Tala's sister Nagam passed her Arabic GCSE with a top grade at the age of thirteen, whilst Yazan's sister Lana, who had arrived recently from Syria, was considered ready by the school at age ten. Thus the Arabic school, like the Chinese school, was adding to children's educational achievement. A certificate awarded to Lana for

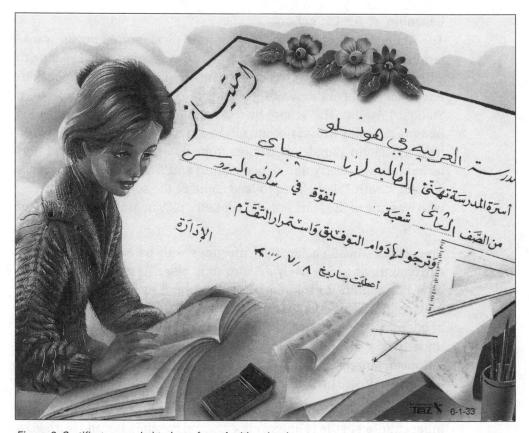

Figure 8: Certificate awarded to Lana from Arabic school.

her end-of-year test pictures the variety of future studies she might anticipate (Figure 8).

Learning at Spanish school

The Latin American Saturday school attended by Brian and Sadhana was established fairly recently in an area of South London where there were many new arrivals from Colombia, Ecuador and Bolivia. The school provided a community focus for these families and for others like those of Sadhana and Brian, who travelled from some distance away. The frequent parties, for occasions ranging from Halloween to summer barbecues, always had activities for children such as games and dressing-up, or sport and dance displays. The school also participated in London-wide events, making costumes and preparing dances for the September carnival procession along the banks of the River Thames.

Dame la mano

Dame la mano y danzaremos;
dame la mano y me amarás.
Como una sola flor seremos,
como una flor y nada más. . .

El mismo verso cantaremos,
al mismo paso bailarás.
Como una espiga ondularemos,
como una espiga y nada más.
Te llamas Rosa y yo Esperanza;
pero tu nombre olvidarás.

Gabriela Mistral.

Figure 9: Poem in Spanish Saturday school textbook by Chilean poet Gabriela Mistral. The first line reads 'Give me your hand and let's dance'.

Saturday mornings were devoted to reading and writing in Spanish. In the afternoon there was a choice of sessions included art, music, dance and chess. For literacy learning, there was a shortage of textbooks and teachers had to photocopy materials. However, the teachers of Sadhana and Brian managed creatively by cutting out pictures from magazines and using these alongside a set of cardboard alphabet letters, and by borrowing dual-language storybooks from the local library so that they could read to the children in Spanish.

Starting with individual letter-sound links, children built up syllables and then words in their writing and reading. At the same time, they listened to longer texts in the stories read by their teachers, and talked about the narrative and their own reactions. Figure 9 shows an example in one of the school textbooks, a poem for children by the famous Chilean poet Gabriela Mistral. The children also performed at Spanish school; Brian's teacher rehearsed a story about animals as a short play for the Christmas party, with the children taking on different roles.

Curriculum activities for the younger children included songs which taught concepts such as numbers, and games involving physical activities linked with learning, such as turning to your left or right hand side. As well as teaching literacy, therefore, the school was reinforcing the conceptual learning that would also be taking place at primary school.

Recognising the importance of community language schools

The children's community language schools complemented their mainstream school learning in several valuable ways.

- **Language learning**: the children were able to study another language, which contributed to their cognitive development (as we see in Chapter Two) and enhanced their future prospects

- **Cultural connections**: the children could maintain links with their family heritage and socialise with peers who shared their cultural background

- **Reinforcing the curriculum**: children's studies gave additional support to their primary school learning in the areas of literacy, numeracy and concept formation

- **Broadening the curriculum**: community schools offered artistic and cultural activities which extended children's learning

The research project with Yazan, Tala, Brian, Sadhana, Ming and Selina opened up each child's biliterate world to their primary school teacher. As the children talked about their languages and demonstrated their knowledge, the primary teachers could see more fully the importance of the learning that was taking place at community school. During the project, the primary and community teachers involved came together to share ideas about the children's literacy education. The primary teachers made it clear that they had come to learn, and their community school colleagues took the floor to explain how they taught Chinese, Arabic and Spanish. As a result, the primary school teachers were able to gain a deeper understanding of what community schools offered, an understanding which they appreciated and continued to use in their work with bilingual children.

Learning at primary school

Although there is a National Curriculum for schools in England, and a National Literacy Strategy which describes how reading and writing should be taught, each primary school interprets these guidelines in particular ways and each class teacher translates them into a variety of different activities. For example, all the schools in the project placed some emphasis on the teaching of phonics, which is considered fundamental in the National Literacy Strategy. Teachers found various ways of drawing children's attention to phoneme-grapheme links.

On the walls of Selina's classroom, for instance, there were posters titled 'Sounds are Fun', showing sound-symbol connections on which the class was currently focusing, such as 'oo' or 'ou', with homemade lists of example words below. Ming's teacher asked the class to sound out words beginning with 'qu', such as 'quit', and then gave several children a letter each, written on a cardboard cut-out 'sock', and requested them to come and stand next to each other in the correct order to make up the word, as if the socks were hanging on a washing line. Tala's teacher invented a poem using the names of all the children in the class in alphabetical order, and they had to find words for objects in the classroom starting with each letter of the alphabet.

Yazan and his classmates matched letters and sounds in alphabetical order, writing each combination on one segment of a drawing of a caterpillar. Sadhana had an 'onset' book, in which she wrote words beginning with particular consonant combinations, each accompanied by a picture: for example, 'tw' for 'twin'. Brian's school had adopted a system for literacy teaching devised in the US, called 'Success for All'. Phonics was taught in an active style involving sounding out the letter whilst drawing it in the air or tracing its outline on a classmate's back.

The Literacy Strategy requires activities to focus on word, sentence and text level. Teachers partly addressed this requirement by giving children structured exercises and worksheets, and partly by asking them to compose their own texts. Often the exercises and composition were based around a key text or theme the class was currently studying, ranging from Magnets and Magnetism to the story of the *Owl Babies* who lost their mother, or a book of nursery rhymes. An example follows from each child's class.

Selina and her classmates designed and wrote postcards about a class trip to the seaside reporting what they had done on the beach. Selina described digging in the sand, picking up shells and playing in the water. The cards included the address of the primary school, and were decorated with a border of seaside-themed items drawn by the children, such as shells, starfish, and buckets and spades.

Ming's class looked at nursery rhyme writing, based around the book *Rhymes to Remember*. The class enjoyed reciting the rhymes, together with actions, and Ming's teacher discussed with them how the endings of words sounded the same to make the rhyme. Children were then given an initial line from a nursery rhyme and asked to write the next one. Ming was unsure what followed the line 'One two three four five' and was advised by one of his classmates that it was 'Once I caught a fish alive'. Using emergent writing, Ming wrote his own version of this and continued the verse to the end.

As part of a topic on The Environment, Tala's teacher read the book *Are You a Spider?* to the whole class, directing them to concentrate on the information given about the characteristics of spiders. The children then wrote their own clues for a guessing game on an animal of their choice: Tala chose a horse and her clues included 'I have a triangle face' and 'I race in TV', each written in Tala's spelling.

The storybook *Owl Babies* provided examples of capital letters and punctuation, focused on by Yazan's teacher as she re-read the story to the class. She also pointed out the speech bubbles in which the baby owls' cry of 'I want my Mummy!' was written. As the story was read aloud, this phrase was repeated by the children each time it occurred in the text. Yazan then tackled the task of matching phrases from the book with speech bubbles for particular characters, and writing each phrase in the correct bubble.

Sadhana's teacher worked with her class on storywriting, emphasising that the purpose of stories is 'to make life interesting and fun'. With the whole class, she discussed how an everyday event such as going shopping could turn into a lively story if something unusual happened. Sadhana's interpretation of this was to write a story about going to the park, where the exciting event was 'I saw my Nanny' from Ecuador. Inspired by this possibility, she wrote quickly and the story developed, involving a visit to the supermarket, the exchange of cards and presents and the return of her grandmother to Ecuador. Sadhana was able to read back her emergent writing to tell the whole story.

Science work on the topic Light and Dark led into a piece of drawing and writing in Brian's class. The children were asked to think how they would describe their house to a visually impaired person, giving directions for moving from one room to another. To gain a feeling for what it would be like to be unable to see, they first had to draw their house with their eyes closed. Brian then wrote about the main external features of his house – it was 'middle size' with a green door and white balcony – and explained how to go up each set of stairs to find the living room and the bathroom.

Multiple learning environments

The descriptions of homes, community schools and primary schools given here are inevitably partial, but provide insight into each as a potential site of learning. In every area of their lives, children encounter a wealth of activities involving literacy, using a variety of texts. Some activities occur informally in the course of everyday life, whilst others – both at home and at school – take place as planned teaching events. However, there is a continuum from informal to formal learning, and the literacy teachers may be siblings or parents as well as teachers in school. In the chapters that follow, we see how Brian, Sadhana, Ming, Selina, Yazan and Tala drew on resources from their different learning environments. Each child re-interpreted the input offered by families, community school teachers and primary school teachers in order to make sense of how writing systems worked.

Ideas for finding out about home and community learning

■ Children may not mention that they are learning another literacy, because they may be unsure how this part of their lives will be seen at primary school. You can show your support and find out which children in your class are becoming biliterate by asking questions as part of informal conversation, such as 'Do you go to another school at weekends or after school? Does your parent/grandparent/sister/brother teach you another language at home?' Opportunities can arise when you see children's re-action to other scripts in the classroom, for example in dual-language storybooks. Asking whether children have a favourite TV programme in a different language can be another way in.

■ To find out more about children's knowledge of written languages, you can encourage them to bring in materials from home. These may be everyday items such as calendars and newspapers, audiovisual materials such as videos, or teaching materials such as textbooks, exercise books and dictionaries. Textbooks may look rather different from English schoolbooks, because there are many ways of learning to read and write which have worked for children throughout the world. If you respond with interest to each item children will gain confidence and will start telling you more about their worlds of learning.

■ Involve all the children in your class in the enjoyment of learning about languages. Children from a monolingual background may well have relatives in other countries, or have been on holiday elsewhere. They may have access to texts in other languages. Even if children have never left their local area, they will have seen multilingual materials in everyday life. You can suggest that they look out for different languages in packaging for toys and food, or instruction leaflets. When they bring these to school, you can ask what they think the languages might be. The next chapter suggests ideas for using multilingual texts in class.

■ Parents – both bilingual and monolingual – may be unsure whether their young children can cope with learning more than one writing system at the same time. You can explain that it is an advantage for children to become aware of different languages and to build on the languages they already have. Languages are being introduced into the primary curriculum because it is beneficial to learn at an early age.

■ The European Language Portfolio is an excellent way of recognising children's language achievements. The Portfolio can be used by all children as a record of their language learning knowledge and experience – from a few words of holiday Spanish to GCSE in Urdu. It is obtainable from CILT (the National Centre for Languages, www.cilt.org.uk) and can be downloaded free from the Resources section of the NACELL website (the National Advisory Centre on Early Language Learning, www. nacell.org.uk). You may want to encourage children by using the Portfolio yourself – you can record what you already know, however small a beginning, and perhaps start learning phrases from languages spoken by children in the class.

■ To celebrate children's learning of other languages and literacies, create a photo display of the children in your class who attend community language school, indicating which language(s) they are learning. Keep the display up to date by asking children to tell you when they have started the next class or won a prize at their community school, and recording these achievements next to the photos. Children's success can also be recognised in whole-school assemblies. Your interest can give status to children's learning and help sustain their efforts, because they are acutely aware of your opinion as their primary school teacher.

■ A display about community language school learning can be permanent and school-wide. Community school events such as Chinese New Year celebrations can be advertised – the schools will be delighted if other families and teachers can attend. To obtain information and publicity material for community language schools, ask children and parents to bring a name and contact telephone number for their school. Headteachers of community schools can then be approached directly – they will be pleased to hear from you.

■ You can offer practical help to support the work of local community schools. A community group may urgently need rooms for Saturday school or after-school classes – can your school provide these, if it is not already doing so? You could invite community school colleagues to observe a lesson with your class – they are keen to find out about different teaching methods. They will also appreciate your interest if you are able to visit their community school and see their classes in action. This could lead to fruitful dialogue about children's learning, drawing on ideas from mainstream and community contexts.

2

Understanding different writing systems

Teachers know that young children work hard to make meaning from each new literacy experience. We see evidence of that work in texts made by children themselves, or in comments overheard during a group task or play in the home corner. Often, though, educators are aware that these are only fragmentary glimpses of a meaning-making process that is ongoing and highly individual.

How can we find out what goes on inside children's minds? How can we encourage biliterate children to show us their thinking as they actively engage with different writing systems? This was the challenge we faced in our research with our six-year-olds who were learning Chinese, Arabic and Spanish at the same time as English.

We decided to ask the children to teach others what they knew. Their 'pupils' would be primary school classmates of their own age, so that they could communicate on a more equal level than with adults. Selecting peers who did not already know Chinese, Arabic or Spanish would mean the child would become the 'teacher', using materials from home or Saturday school as a resource.

Peer teaching

With the help of each child's primary school teacher, a quiet place for peer teaching was found, ranging from the school library to the staff room. There was no shortage of volunteer pupils – many children wanted to be the first to learn to write in Chinese, Arabic or Spanish. Some even asked for homework and brought it back for inspection.

As a basis for teaching, the bilingual children brought their community language work with them, often in a small backpack used for Saturday school. I provided additional materials borrowed from homes or community language schools, such as Chinese New Year banners, exercise books with squared grids from Chinese school, alphabet teaching materials in Spanish, or work done at home with siblings in Arabic. Plain and lined paper and a variety of pens, pencils and erasers were also supplied, and sometimes the children could use a whiteboard to demonstrate writing.

The peer teaching sessions had an open-ended format and were mainly directed by the children themselves. With the materials mentioned above as a resource, the children were encouraged to show their 'pupils' how to write in Chinese, Arabic or Spanish. Sometimes I asked them to explain a particular point, if this had not arisen spontaneously.

Each of our young 'teachers' also demonstrated aspects of their writing system to the whole class, in sessions that ran from ten minutes to an hour and a half. As thirty children sat on the carpet with clipboards, concentrating hard on producing unfamiliar symbols, the fascination of finding out about different scripts was obvious. Meanwhile, we gained insight into the ideas Yazan, Tala, Ming, Selina, Brian and Sadhana had accrued from their biliterate experience.

Children learning from the world around them

We examined the children's learning from a social semiotic perspective, looking at how individuals make meaning from the sign systems used in their social environment. Every society develops a variety of sign systems – speech, visual images, writing – to communicate ideas. Children encounter writing as one of these sign systems, and they have to figure out how this particular system works. Biliterate children discover not only that marks on paper or screen represent language, but also that the marks may look different or operate in different ways for different languages.

In their quest for understanding, children observe how people around them make and use a variety of texts: birthday cards, family letters, TV guides, newspapers, take-away food menus. They also receive formal and informal teaching from adults and other children, drawing their attention to certain aspects of written language. Each child brings together the information offered to them, and engages in a continual process of working out what symbols stand for and how they are used.

Gunther Kress (1997, 2000) has shown how children go about this process of interpretation. When reading a text or designing their own text, each child has an *interest* as an individual sign-user growing up in a particular social environment. For example, a four-year-old may be concerned with how her name, Emily, can be represented in writing. She has been paying attention to the versions produced by people around her, and has begun to understand that E and other letters can stand for sounds in her name. She has built up certain *representational resources* which she can currently use – her ability to write particular letters, and her understanding of issues such as directionality and spacing. Every time Emily writes her name over a period of more than a year, she investigates and develops these different aspects of representation.

So children do not simply absorb input from those around them. They actively re-interpret this input, a process which Kress calls *transformation*. As they produce their own texts or read the texts of others, children engage in transformative thinking. We shall see this taking place in the comments and writing of Selina, Ming, Tala, Yazan, Sadhana and Brian as they consider how their different script systems operate. We also see how the children's ideas develop by first identifying a key issue, then building on it and clarifying it.

Knowledge about language

Bilingual children tend to compare their language systems, thinking about how they are similar to each other and how they differ. As a result, young bilinguals often have a heightened awareness of how language works. This metalinguistic awareness has been found in a number of research studies about bilingual children, discussed by Ellen Bialystok (2001). Some researchers, including Ludo Verhoeven (1994) and Daniel Wagner (1993), have focused on biliteracy and found that literacy learning skills can be transferred between different writing systems.

Metalinguistic awareness can begin at an early age. Four-year-old Meera, who I observed in her London nursery class (Kenner, 2000), commented on a poster about her favourite Bollywood video, written by her mother in Gujerati with an English translation. One part of the poster contained three words in Gujerati – the names of the main characters in the film – with only two words in English below. Meera realised that the Gujerati and English versions should correspond to each other, and asked 'Why three?' It turned out that her mother had been uncertain about how to write the third name in English.

Language awareness can be fostered by explicitly teaching about difference. This is common in community language schools, where teachers recognise that their pupils are growing up in a bilingual world and help them to compare language systems. Research in Gujerati schools in Leicester, England by Arvind Bhatt and Nirmala Bhojani (Martin *et al*, 2004) shows teachers explaining grammatical differences between English and Gujerati. Leena Helavaara Robertson (2004) found a similar approach in Urdu classes in Watford, north of London, where children discussed with their teacher how sounds in English words related to those in Urdu.

In this chapter we see examples of metalinguistic awareness being demonstrated by the six children who took part in our project, helped by the explanations given by their teachers in Chinese, Arabic and Spanish school.

Chinese: Selina and Ming
Chinese is not alphabetic

The Chinese writing system operates on a wholly different basis to English. Chinese is mainly logographic, not alphabetic. Instead of using letters to represent sounds, Chinese uses characters which represent ideas. So a character – or sometimes a pair of characters – might stand for 'book' or 'read', for example. Most characters contain two parts: a semantic radical which gives a clue to the meaning and a phonetic radical which gives a clue to the sound. Each character is made up of a combination of strokes and has a pattern which children learn to recognise, distinguishing it from other characters which look similar but have a different meaning.

Ming and Selina realised that Chinese and English writing worked in different ways. When I asked 'Does Chinese have an alphabet?', Ming thought for a moment and then shook his head. Selina's reply to the same question was 'No, just numbers'. Her answer shows an understanding of the different bases on which symbol systems can operate. The number system in Chinese contains a defined set of symbols (representing 1–10) which can be combined to create every possible number, just as a set of alphabetic letters can be combined to create every possible word. Chinese writing, however, is an open-ended system which involves a great many different characters.

Often there is a one-to-one relationship between an English word and a Chinese character, as Ming asserted one day when teaching his primary school class about Chinese writing. He wrote the Chinese character for 'letter' (a letter which would be delivered through the post) on the board, with the English word 'letter' next to it. One of Ming's classmates asked about the Chinese character 'What does that word mean?' Ming replied 'This is 'letter', English 'letter' [referring to the English version] and you write it in Chinese like this'. Ming saw no problem with the idea of having an equivalent Chinese version of an English word.

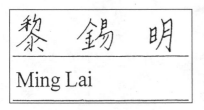

Figure 10: Ming's name in Chinese (Lai Sei Ming) and English.

Ming also understood that the building blocks for English writing are alphabetic letters, whereas Chinese is based on characters. He pointed to the front of his Chinese school exercise book (Figure 10), where his name was written using three characters: 'Lai Sei Ming' (Chinese names begin with the surname), observing 'That one's got three words and the English one's got four'. He went on to explain about his English name, 'Ming Lai', 'I got some different ones ... Ming is four, seven if it's together'. So Ming was pointing out that in English his name was made up of letters – four for 'Ming' and seven for 'Ming Lai', but his Chinese name consisted of three characters, one for each word.

Although Ming only knew how to read and write a few Chinese characters at this time, he had developed ideas about the basis of the entire system as compared to English. We did not see these ideas being mentioned in Chinese school, though they were implied in the teaching. When children were practising a new character, the teacher usually wrote the equivalent English word above it, but did not discuss the distinction between alphabetic and logographic systems. However, Ming was evidently thinking about this difference.

Understanding Chinese characters

A few Chinese characters have a direct visual link to the idea they represent. For example, the character for 'mountain' looks as though it contains three 'peaks', and the character for 'cry' has dots which look like tears descending from two squares which look like eyes. The teachers at Chinese school sometimes pointed out this link. But most characters are not pictorial in such a simple way, and Ming realised this. When he was teaching his classmate Amina, she tried to represent 'mouth' in Chinese by drawing an oval shape. Ming strongly dismissed her efforts by saying 'That's wrong, she has to write in Chinese, not draw pictures!'

(五)

秋天

秋天天氣涼，
地上落葉多。

暖

春天

夏天

5

Figure 11: Passage about 'Autumn' from Selina's Chinese school textbook. The character I have ringed means 'autumn'. The right-hand part of this character stands for 'fire', and the left-hand part for 'crops'. The origin may lie in the burning of crop stubble in autumn.

As it happens, the Chinese character for mouth is a rectangle, a stylized version of an oval shape, but Ming's point was that Chinese is not a system simply based on pictures.

To understand Chinese characters, children have to learn to recognise stroke patterns which represent ideas in a more abstract way. It can be helpful to look for the semantic radical within a character – the pattern which gives a clue to the meaning. For example, the symbol which means 'fire' also appears in a number of related characters such as 'lamp'. Selina's mother would tell her the meaning of these different elements, and Selina herself then searched for the symbols she recognised within characters. She pointed out to me that the symbol for 'fire' was part of the character for 'autumn', shown on a page from her Chinese school textbook (Figure 11).

Ming also knew that the 'fire' symbol could appear in other characters. He particularly enjoyed writing this symbol and demonstrated a character containing it in a peer teaching session, saying as he wrote 'This is the fire one, yeah, fire's in it'. His older sister showed him the symbol for 'water' and asked if he could find it in the characters in his Chinese textbook. Ming rose to the challenge, looked through the whole book and announced 'Only two fires and three waters'.

Selina knew that Chinese characters could contain parts that represent sound as well as parts that represent meaning. This issue comes to the fore when writing a Chinese version of an English personal name. The new Chinese characters can be made up from symbols which stand for sounds – a transliteration. Another approach is to use symbols that represent the meaning of the English word. The two approaches can also be combined, drawing on both meaning and sound. When Selina was going to teach Chinese to her friend Ruby at primary school, Selina's mother suggested writing Ruby's name in Chinese. She showed Selina two ways of doing this (Figure 12). The first way, shown on the right of Ruby's

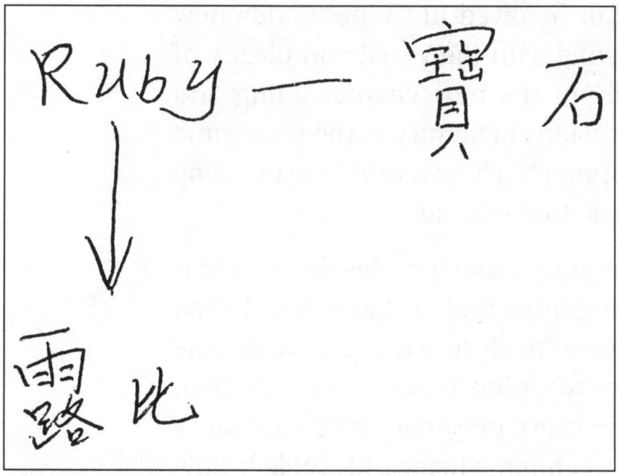

Figure 12: Selina's mother showed two possible ways of representing the name 'Ruby' in Chinese: as 'precious stone' (right-hand side) or 'Loo-bi' (below).

English name, was to use the characters 'precious' and 'stone' to represent the meaning of 'ruby'. Another way, shown below, was to write characters which would give the nearest sound, 'Loo-bi'.

Selina then explained these different possibilities to Ruby. She pointed to the characters for 'precious' and 'stone' and told her friend 'You're a diamond, yeah, and the diamond turns into a stone, and the stone is a lot of money'. This statement showed that Selina saw how the idea of 'ruby' was similar to that of 'diamond', and that 'diamond' could be made up of two concepts, 'stone' and 'valuable'. Being able to analyse the meanings which together make up a new idea is an important aspect of reading in Chinese. Selina followed this by pointing to the second way her mother had written 'Ruby' and saying 'and this is your translator, it's Loo-bi'. She understood that this was the Chinese equivalent for the sounds involved.

Looking for meanings in Chinese

Learning Chinese writing involves different challenges from learning English, stretching children's minds in different ways. To someone brought up with English, Chinese may seem more difficult, but this is probably because we are used to one system and find it hard to comprehend another that works on such a different basis. The alphabetic system is simpler in some ways; Selina remarked to her mother that English was easy because you could use spelling but Chinese was hard because there were so many meanings behind the characters. On the other hand, the richness of metaphor involved in Chinese adds new dimensions to children's learning, along with the visual complexity of the characters, discussed more fully in the next chapter. Ming and Selina were experiencing these dimensions of literacy at the same time as their learning of the alphabetic approach. They were able to examine the written world from both angles – a double benefit.

Selina enjoyed looking for the meanings in characters, despite her complaints that Chinese was 'harder'. Her mother told us that at first, Selina asked why her Chinese name was so difficult to write. But when she heard that it contained the character meaning 'precious' or 'valuable', she was happy to write it. In Chinese every personal name includes a character which contains a wider meaning, whereas in English only some personal names have a literal meaning; Ruby happens to be an example, and Selina pointed out the symbol for 'precious' occurring in both their names as written in Chinese.

Selina began to look for the 'precious' symbol elsewhere, and found it in a decorative New Year banner at home saying 'Wealth is coming', on a Chinese cushion, and on jewellery in her local department store. She was fascinated to see a character from her name appear in other contexts, and recognised this as an aspect of Chinese not often found in English. So when I asked her 'Is Chinese different from English?' she chose this example to reply 'Yes, English people are not the same as Chinese people because when I went to a shop with my mum I saw some Chinese writing and I saw my name in the middle'.

Another special attribute of Chinese writing is that it can be used to represent different spoken Chinese languages. It is a shared communication system for people from different parts of China, who use languages that vary as much as European languages do. Selina was aware of this flexibility because she spoke both Cantonese and Mandarin at home and her mother was teaching her to write Chinese through the medium of both languages. In her hour-long Chinese lesson with her mother every evening, Selina practised reading out passages from her textbook in Cantonese and then in Mandarin. When she showed her Chinese name to Ruby, she read the writing out in two ways: "bo boy', this is 'bau bei' as well" (the first was the pronunciation in Cantonese and the second in Mandarin). When asked 'What's the difference?', she replied 'Nothing'. She recognised that the characters stood for equivalent meanings in both languages.

Arabic: Tala and Yazan
A different directionality
One of the most obvious differences between Arabic and English is directionality: Arabic goes from right to left and English from left to right. Yazan demonstrated that he knew Arabic and English books went in different directions. Showing his Arabic school textbook in a peer teaching session, he pointed to the front cover and stated 'Not the end'. Turning to the back cover, he emphasised 'This is the end'. And to make sure his audience was completely clear about the matter, he pointed to the front cover again and said 'This is the first'.

Yazan's explanation shows that he understood both systems – the Arabic and the English one. He also realised that his classmates would probably only know one system of directionality, from left to right, so he needed to make the difference explicit for them. In doing so, Yazan was drawing on the advice given by his teachers in Arabic school, who often told their pupils 'Arabic – right to left, English – left to right'.

As well as knowing about directionality at the macro-level (for a whole book), children also need to understand the micro-directionality of lines on the page. Tala was fully aware of this. When she was teaching her primary school 'pupils' to write the Arabic word 'mama' (mum), they produced symbols which looked like hers but written from left to right. Tala did not accept their efforts, because the directionality was incorrect. She told them 'No, that's wrong ... we don't start from there, we start from here!', pointing to the right-hand side of the page. She put an arrow on the right-hand side of the paper to act as a reminder (Figure 13), just as her teacher sometimes did at Arabic school.

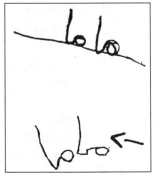

Figure 13: Arrow used by Tala to remind her classmates to start on the right when writing in Arabic.

So for Tala, directionality was a key characteristic of Arabic writing. When she was teaching her whole class at primary school, I asked her to tell them the most important thing to remember about Arabic, and she said 'Start the other way'. She even made me turn over my notebook and start from the back page when I was writing about her Arabic learning at home, thus pointing out in a humorous way that I needed to give my note-taking an Arabic dimension.

Understanding directionality

Yazan was figuring out the concept of micro-directionality (for lines on a page), as shown by his comments and actions over time. At the beginning of the school year he did not correct his 'pupils' if they wrote Arabic from left to right in peer teaching sessions, but by the end of the year he would do so. When his final pupil was about to begin her writing he announced: 'The Arabic starts from here', pointing to the top right-hand corner of the page.

During the year, Yazan demonstrated that he knew directionality was an issue – one that he was working on, but had not yet resolved. In a primary school English literacy task he asked me 'Which side shall we start? I think this side', pointing to the right-hand side of the page. Although he was wrong in this case, he was obviously thinking about the matter and was aware that there were two alternatives. He was seeking advice from me, just as he did from his older sister Lana when she was giving him a spelling test in English and in Arabic – he asked her which side of the page he should write the numbers for the test.

In my final observation of Yazan at Arabic school, he was able to self-correct. Having started to write an arithmetical sum in Arabic from left to right, he commented 'Oops, I did it wrong way' and rubbed it out, starting again from the right-hand corner of the page. Thus we can see how a child identifies an issue as significant when learning about writing – in this case directionality – and clarifies the issue by thinking it over and making use of help from others. In time, the child arrives at a more detailed understanding of the concept, though each child's pathway to learning may be slightly different.

Joined-up writing in Arabic

Arabic, like English, has an alphabet. As well as becoming familiar with this alphabet and finding out which letter represents which sound, there is something else learners of Arabic need to know when they begin reading and writing. All Arabic words consist of letters joined to one another. Because of this writing process, each letter may have a different form when it begins a word, or when it joins to other letters in the middle or joins at the end of the word. These forms are known as the initial, medial and final forms and may look different from the letter's appearance in the alphabet. So each letter can have up to four different forms, and children have to learn how to recognise and produce all of them. In addition, there are six letters which cannot join to the left, sometimes called the 'stubborn' letters, and children have to know which these are.

An example can be seen in a page from Yazan's Arabic school exercise book (Figure 14). The letter 'ha', which represents the sound 'h', is illustrated by a picture of a pigeon, 'hamama' in Arabic. There is then an opportunity to practise the form of 'ha' as it appears in the alphabet, on several lines below. Then three words are given, each containing the sound 'h': 'hafila' (bus), 'mahbas' (ring) and 'muftah' (key). The task is to identify the letter 'ha' in each written word. Reading from right to left, 'ha' occurs at the beginning in 'hafila', in the middle in 'mahbas', and at the end in 'muftah'. At the beginning and in the middle of the word, 'ha' takes the form of the top part of the alphabet letter. At the end of the word 'muftah', it appears in the same form as the alphabet letter, but this is because the previous letter is one of the few which cannot join to the left. So 'ha' has to start again, and since it is the final letter it stands alone, in its full form.

Figure 14: Words with the letter 'ha' (sound 'h') in Arabic 'Hamama' (pigeon), 'hafila' (bus), 'mahbas' (ring), 'muftah' (key).

In Arabic school children were introduced to these ideas in the beginners' class, because it is impossible to read or write without understanding the principles of joined-up writing. The teacher showed words together with a picture clue, with the initial, medial or final letter highlighted in a different colour. Children were asked to identify which letter it was. In their own writing, children made use of the different letter forms. As the year progressed, they learned how to deconstruct whole words into their constituent letters, and by the second year many children were becoming proficient at this skill.

Tala showed her primary school friends how letters changed form when joined in writing. She wrote her name in Arabic, and then ringed the letters she had used from the alphabet chart (Figure 15). She explained to her classmates that the letters in the written word looked different 'because I joined them up'. Showing them again, she wrote her name and said 'Isn't it there's a T in Arabic like this, yeah?' (pointing to the letter which stands for the sound 't' on the alphabet chart). She then began writing her name once more and as she began the 't' she observed 'and now I change it, because Arabic is magic'. As she added the letters which represent the 'l' and 'a' sounds she pointed out with an air of supreme confidence 'and now I just join the L and join the A'. (Note: I have used capital letters to represent letter-names, and lower-case letters to represent letter sounds. When describing the children's writing, I have used capitals or lower-case depending on the choice they made).

Tala was drawing on input from many lessons at Arabic school, and she was adding her own sense of the special properties held by Arabic script. In her words 'and now I change it, because Arabic is magic' she imaginatively evoked the process whereby a letter mutates from one form into another, and her feeling of power as an independent writer.

Tala went on to write her friend's name 'Tina' in Arabic, a word she had never written before. As she wrote, she chose the letters required and worked out the relevant form of each letter for its position in the word. She showed the same ability when writing down items for an 'Arabic menu' as part of a play activity at home. At the age of six, Tala understood the principles behind joined-up writing and had developed considerable knowledge about different letter forms.

Yazan was also becoming familiar with the process of deconstructing Arabic words into separate letters. This was one of the tasks he practised

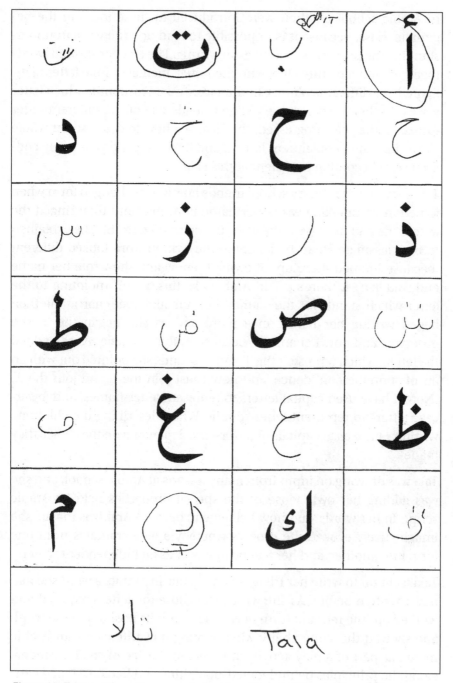

Figure 15: Tala's writing of her name in Arabic, with part of the alphabet chart where she has ringed the letters used: 'ta', 'alif' and 'lam'.

with the help of his sister Lana. Using a small whiteboard kept in her bedroom for the purposes of her teaching role, Lana wrote Arabic words and asked Yazan to tell her the letters which appeared in each one. With a little help from Lana, Yazan was able to identify the letters in words including 'arnab' (rabbit), 'asad' (lion) and 'mama' (mum). At Arabic school, he found particular letters within words when asked by his teacher.

Grammatical issues in Arabic

Arabic has different masculine and feminine forms for verb endings and children are taught to recognise these. This point of grammar, like many others, was taught in the Arabic school in the context of reading. Tala's textbook contained a picture of a family activity on each page, accompanied by statements about what was happening in the picture. Amongst the characters the children came to know over the course of the book were a sister and brother, Reem and Khalid. In one of her Arabic lessons, Tala pointed out the feminine and masculine verb endings in statements about Reem and Khalid. She showed me these again when I visited her at home, writing 'For mail [i.e. male] is this later [i.e. letter]' alongside the male verb ending in Arabic and 'For femail is this later' alongside the female verb ending (Figure 16). Just in case I had not fully grasped the concept, she emphasised it by writing 'femail is a girl' and 'mail is a boy'.

Learning Arabic therefore raised a number of issues for Yazan and Tala to consider that did not arise when learning English. Directionality was only one of these. Using an alphabetic script that looked different and operated on different rules from English required children to think carefully about the principles behind writing systems.

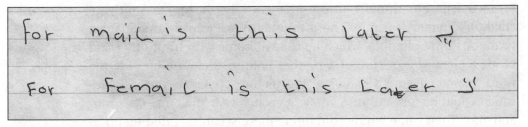

Figure 16: Tala explaining the use of male and female affixes in Arabic.

Spanish: Sadhana and Brian
Vowels and syllables

Spanish and English are both alphabetic and use the same script and directionality. They are certainly more similar than Chinese and English, or Arabic and English. However, when watching Brian and Sadhana learning in Spanish school we became aware that there are important differences in the teaching of the two writing systems.

First is how letters are taught. In Spanish, the vowels are taught first, rather than approaching the alphabet from A to Z. This is because Spanish is phonetically regular and each vowel has only one sound, unlike English where vowels can have many possible sounds. Vowels are seen as playing a key role in Spanish because, as the teachers at Spanish school said, 'they give sound to the words'. So children first learn 'a,e,i,o,u', and teachers try to find many ways of making these letters memorable. One example is the page from Sadhana's Saturday school work (Figure 17) called 'El viento de las vocales' (The wind of the vowels), in which the vowels are seen merrily blowing about.

Sadhana was aware that letters were taught differently in her English school and her Spanish school. When I brought the page 'El viento de las vocales' for her to use in a peer teaching session, she became excited, saying 'Las vocales!' When I offered her a set of cardboard alphabet letters and suggested she put them in order, she realised that there were two possible ways of doing so, and asked 'ABCD or a,e,i,o,u?' (saying ABCD as English letter names and giving the vowels their Spanish pronunciation).

In Spanish school, vowels were next linked up with consonants to form syllables, which could then be built into words. The first consonant used was 'm', which can be combined with 'a' to make the word 'mamá' (mum). This emotionally important word is chosen to motivate children's literacy learning. The introductory page in Brian's Spanish textbook from Colombia, which he used at home with his mother and brother, showed a picture of a mother holding a child alongside the word 'mamá' (Figure 18). Below the picture appeared the syllables which could be formed from 'm' with each vowel: 'ma', 'me', 'mi', 'mo', and 'mu'. Then came words containing these syllables, building up to the sentence 'mi mamá me ama' (my mum loves me).

Brian and his classmates practised saying the syllables 'ma', 'me', 'mi', 'mo', and 'mu' many times. They often heard their teacher explaining –

Figure 17: 'El viento de las vocales' (the wind of the vowels): pictures to teach vowel sounds from Spanish school textbook.

Figure 18: From Brian's Spanish primer: forming syllables by combining the letter 'm'
with each of the five vowels, building up to 'mi mamá me ama' (my mum loves me).

always in Spanish – the principle of joining 'm' and 'a' to make 'ma'. She told them that letters without a vowel attached did not have a sound of their own. Brian then explained this principle to his English primary school class. He showed them the page concerning 'mamá' in his Spanish book and told them (in English) 'The M on her own doesn't say anything – just 'mmm' – you have to put it together'. He pointed to the syllable 'ma' and said 'That's formed with the 'a' – with 'a' it makes ma.'

Brian's explanation involved translating his teacher's idea from Spanish into English. This showed that he understood the concept she was putting across. He also expressed himself in quite a sophisticated way, saying 'That's formed with the 'a'..', which indicates that he was thinking about how language works and could use metalinguistic terminology.

Same letter, different sound

Some letters sound the same in Spanish or in English, such as 'm'. However, other letters sound different, such as 'i' in Spanish, which sounds like the letter-name 'E' in English. Children have to work out these differences and remember to pay particular attention to such letters.

Teachers at Spanish school were aware that their pupils would need special help with this task. They found ways of highlighting the Spanish letter 'i' by giving it a special name, so that children did not use the English letter-name 'E' instead. If Brian's teacher saw children writing 'pela' instead of 'pila', for example, she would remind them about 'la 'i' con sombrerito' (the 'i' with the little hat, the 'hat' being the dot which characterises this letter). She explained to me that children growing up in a bilingual situation benefit from such help, and that how the reminder is given 'depends on the creativity of each teacher'.

Parents and other family members teaching their children at home also worked out ways of approaching the 'E/i' distinction. Sadhana's mother characterised the Spanish 'i' as 'la 'i' con palito y bolita' (the 'i' with the little stick and the little ball). Brian's mother, grandmother and older brother helped him by emphasising the 'i' sound whenever he was writing a word containing it.

Over the year, Brian and Sadhana clarified the distinction between the English letter-name 'E' and the Spanish letter 'i' for themselves, with the aid of teachers and family. One evening, Brian was using a set of cardboard alphabet letters at home to make words in Spanish. He produced 'neño' instead of 'niño' ('boy'), and when his grandmother reminded him he changed 'e' to 'i'. The next day Brian was using the same set of letters in a peer teaching session at primary school. Looking for the Spanish vowels, he said 'Donde está el 'e'?' (Where is the 'e'? – giving that vowel its Spanish pronunciation). He picked up the letter 'i', said 'e' and then changed his mind, stating 'i' with the correct Spanish pronunciation. Here he showed that the letters 'e' and 'i' were connected in his thinking, and that he was working out the sound-symbol distinction in each writing system. Later in the same teaching session, when Brian's friend Charlie asked him why he had pointed to the letter 'i' and called it 'E', Brian announced confidently: 'Because it's Spanish – it's different!'

Sadhana sometimes wrote the letter 'E' to represent the Spanish sound 'i'. However, she also showed that she was figuring out this difference between her two writing systems. When she was arranging a set of alphabet letters in the sequence of the English alphabet, she asked her mother to pass her the letter 'E'. Her mother thought she was working in Spanish and offered 'i'. But Sadhana replied 'No!' and started singing the well-known English primary school song beginning 'ABCDEFG' to signal that she was dealing with the English alphabet, not the Spanish one.

On the same day, Sadhana showed me a book to teach writing in Spanish, brought by her mother from Ecuador. She commented 'Es que hay muchos 'i's y 'u's' (The thing is that there are lots of 'i's and 'u's). There were in fact many examples of all five vowels to practise, and here Sadhana had singled out the two vowels most different from English ('u' in Spanish is pronounced 'oo', which is an uncommon pronunciation of 'u' in English). She pronounced both Spanish vowels correctly.

Subtle differences in pronunciation

The letter 'm' sounds the same in English and Spanish, but some other letters – including 'p' and 't' – have a slightly different pronunciation. When 'p' and 't' come at the beginning of words and syllables in Spanish, they have a heavier sound than in English. For example, in the word 'pato' (duck) the 'p' almost sounds like 'b' in English, and the 't' almost like 'd'. A similar effect happens with the Spanish 'c' at the beginning of some words and syllables, where it sounds like 'g'.

Sadhana was particularly sensitive to differences in pronunciation. She insisted that her English primary school classmates repeated Spanish words until she was satisfied with the way they spoke. She also noticed

Figure 19: Sadhana's writing of 'foca' (seal), originally beginning 'fog'.

differences between Latin American dialects of Spanish. Her own family spoke Ecuadorian Spanish, and on one occasion she told me 'I speak in Colombia – the Colombia speak like this'. She proceeded to imitate a conversation by talking into the telephone at home.

Sadhana showed her awareness of the particular sounds of 'p', 't' and 'c' in Spanish through her own writing. When writing the word 'pelícano' (pelican), she began with 'b' until her mother corrected her. She also began 'foca' (seal) with the letters 'fog' (Figure 19), and wrote 'conejo' (rabbit) as 'gonejo'. She was using the letters 'b' and 'g' to represent the heavier sounds she could hear in those words.

Sadhana's method of writing these sounds was unusual but consistent. Several months earlier, at a time when she was developing the idea of sound-symbol connections, she was already using 'b' for the Spanish 'p', 'd' for 't' and 'g' for 'c'. We can see this in the following list of words she wrote. I have underlined the relevant letters in each case. Sadhana's highlighting of these particular sounds is all the more striking because not all the symbols in her emergent writing yet represented sounds (for example, she included many 'n's in her words, although they do not seem to stand for the sound 'n'). Her emphasis on using 'b', 'd' and 'g' suggests that Sadhana had already identified these 'sounds of difference', which stood out to her as a bilingual learner.

Standard spelling	As written by Sadhana
casa	gsan
tortuga	dondgn
pescado	besgana
gato	gdon
cama	gnma

Sadhana had experienced a great deal of input concerning letter-sound relationships both at Spanish school and English school. However, nobody had suggested to her that she should write 'conejo' as 'gonejo'. This was Sadhana's own way of using the alphabetic principle. It shows that children can adapt principles for their own purposes, and once again reminds us that each child finds their individual pathway into writing.

Children's capacities to learn

From the evidence described here, we can see that six-year-olds are capable of dealing with different writing systems. They are not disconcerted by difference, as adults may be once they have become accustomed to one kind of system. Children are busy investigating the world of graphic symbols around them, and their approach is flexible. They are prepared to accept the variety of concepts on which each system is based.

At times in the course of the research project, we saw that the children's knowledge about their other writing system caused them to try to explain ideas English adults found difficult to understand. When Selina was teaching Chinese to her primary school class, she used a sheet of writing prepared by her mother as a guide. One sentence, written in both Chinese and English, was 'parents want children to do good learning'. As Selina watched her friend Ruby writing the first part of the Chinese character for 'learning', she commented 'it's half a word'. The class teacher and I struggled to comprehend what 'half a word' meant, and Selina tried to help us by saying 'you make a new word'.

To understand Selina's point, I sought clarification later from a friend who studied Chinese at university. In a lengthy conversation, she explained that some Chinese characters are made up of two parts which both contribute to the meaning but which may not be able to stand alone. This is why Selina referred to 'half a word'. Although we do not know if she yet understood this concept completely, she was gaining a sense of it from discussions with her mother. Meanwhile, as I tried to grasp the idea myself, my friend said kindly 'English people often take a long time to understand this'.

Children may be forming their ideas about writing systems before they have the vocabulary to fully explain them. When Ming was comparing the writing of his name in Chinese and English, he made the comment 'I got some different ones'. What he meant was that the symbols used in each system were different: Chinese writing uses characters while English uses alphabetic letters. Some of that vocabulary would have been difficult for a six-year-old to use, but Ming understood the underlying concept.

Tala came across a similar challenge over vocabulary when she was showing her classmates how to write her brother's name, Khalid, in Arabic. She pointed out that there was a gap in the middle of the Arabic word. This is because the letter which represents the sound 'a' is one of the 'stubborn letters' which cannot join to the left. So 'Khalid' is written in two parts, 'Kha' and 'lid', with a small gap between them. Tala explained it in this way:

> 'Can I tell you something? You know this and this [pointing to each part of the word] – they're not actually together. They have to be split up. This [circling the first part] says 'Khal', and this [circling the second part] says 'lid'. 'Khal' is one word and 'lid' is another one word'.

Although Tala used the 'l' sound twice, it's clear that she was trying to explain the principle of leaving a gap between parts of a word when a letter could not join to others. She did not think that 'Khal' and 'lid' were two separate words. Earlier in the same session she had put a ring round the whole word 'Khalid' and announced 'We've done that one now'. Rather, she did not have another term to use for these separate units which together make up an Arabic word – especially since this formation does not occur in English. Tala's thoughts were running ahead of the language she had at her disposal to express them.

Stimulating language awareness

Dealing with different writing systems can sharpen children's ideas about how language works. We see this explicitly in Ming's statement 'I got some different ones' about his name written in Chinese and English, or in Brian's explanation of why he had pointed to the letter 'i' and pronounced it like the English letter-name 'E': 'Because it's Spanish – it's different!' A similar process of comparison underlies many of the children's comments and actions described above.

It is striking that the children began to understand the principles of Chinese, Arabic and Spanish writing as well as English, even though they only studied their community language for a few hours a week compared to learning English every weekday at primary school. This suggests that language awareness develops quite quickly if children have the chance to encounter other writing systems.

The children's primary school classmates were also keen to investigate Chinese, Arabic or Spanish in the peer teaching sessions. Ming's first pupil was Amina, who was initially disconcerted by Chinese characters being so different from English. When Ming showed her how to write the Chinese number two she said 'No ... that's not two!' But she soon began to realise that this new system could include elements that looked rather like geometric shapes. She used her idea to improvise when Ming gave her a 'test' at the end of the lesson, and asked her to write several words which he had not yet taught her. Amina produced a different shape to represent each word, starting with the Chinese symbols Ming had shown her for 'ten' (which looks like a cross) and 'mouth' (a square), and continuing with a triangle, a half-moon shape and so on.

When Jack was learning Spanish with Brian, he quickly picked up the different pronunciation of the letter 'i'. The two boys were making word-searches for their class, in which the task was to find Spanish words within a grid of letters. Jack commented with amusement that if his classmates found the word 'mi', they would not know how to pronounce it.

Children in Yazan's primary school class noticed that the symbol '0' (which stands for the number 'five' in Arabic) looks like zero in English. However, they rapidly accepted that it represented 'five' in Arabic. Yazan demonstrated an example of subtraction in Arabic, writing the numbers for '10–5' from right to left. A child called out the correct answer 'five', having dealt with the different directionality, deciphered the numbers, and worked it out.

Particularly in a multilingual city like London, primary school children are often aware of each other's languages and enjoy trying them out informally. Maya, when being taught by Ming, referred to this kind of experience. She knew that her friend Ling had a Chinese teacher and when Ming recited some numbers, Maya recognised the sounds and said 'Ling can count to ten in Chinese'. She also told us that Ling had taught her how to say 'vampire' in Chinese!

However, this informal exchange with friends is often the only opportunity children have to find out about different languages at school. In comparison, the six children in our project experienced rich contact with different writing systems. There were moments when they emphasised that their peers did not have this advantage. When Tala's classmate Emily wrote an Arabic word from left to right, Tala rubbed the word out and admonished her friend – half-teasing, half-serious – 'Don't you even know how to do *anything* yet, Emily?' And when Brian's friend Charlie kept asking why he had pointed to the letter 'i' and called it 'E', even though Brian had already explained 'it's Spanish – it's different!', Brian commented 'It's going to take him a long time'. He realised that Charlie was only accustomed to one language and one writing system and might find it difficult to widen his horizons.

The interest shown by the 'pupils' in the peer teaching sessions highlights children's common desire to learn about different writing systems. The work they produced and the questions they asked their young teachers shows their potential to benefit from this opportunity – a point to which I shall return.

But first we see how Brian, Sadhana, Yazan, Tala, Ming and Selina took an alert approach to figuring out how English worked, as well as being able to teach their classmates about Spanish, Arabic or Chinese. Examples follow of how each of them dealt with a writing task at primary school.

Figuring out writing in English
Brian: 'My house is middle size'

When Brian's class was studying Light and Dark in a science lesson, children were asked to write down ideas for describing their home to a visually impaired person and giving directions to move from one room to another. Brian decided to begin with 'my house is middle size'. He wrote 'My haus in' and corrected 'in' to 'is'. For the words 'middle size' he produced 'midor sias': an attempt to accurately represent the sounds that are heard when these words are spoken in London English (the 'l' in 'middle' disappears and the vowel sound in 'size' is lengthened).

Next Brian wrote 'green dor'. He checked the spelling of 'green' with a classmate and self-corrected 'dor' to 'door', saying 'two O's'. The following phrase – 'the balcony is white' – took a good deal of thought, with several changes to the word 'balcony' as he tried to represent the first syllable (which has another disappearing 'l' sound in London English). He tried 'baw', but eventually settled for 'the bakine is wit'.

Brian's instructions for getting around the house were 'go up the stairs to the living room' and 'go up more stairs and go in the bathroom'. He wrote this as 'go ap teh stes teh leven rum' and 'go up mor stes and go in teh bav rum'. Again, he made corrections as he wrote, altering a letter 's' which had been written back-to-front and changing 'bov' to 'bav'. Although his final version was not exactly orthodox, we can see that Brian was still trying to write the sounds he heard: the characteristic 'v' (or 'f') sound for 'th' in the London English version of 'bath', and the shortened vowel sound in 'room'. As often happens in children's emergent writing, Brian's knowledge of the correct way to write 'the' – which he used earlier in the piece – co-existed with other versions at this point, just as 'up' appeared correctly and also as 'ap'.

Gunther Kress's research on early spelling (2000) shows how children make every effort to accurately represent the sounds they hear, using the resources currently available to them. Sadhana's writing of particular sounds in Spanish demonstrates this effort, and here Brian applied a similar aim to writing London English. Children also use visual strategies, as Brian did when correcting his writing of 'door' and remembering that it had 'two Os'. Knowledge can take time to settle, as with Brian's different versions of 'the' and 'up'. If we pay careful attention to the actual writing process, we can see evidence of the thinking going on behind children's decisions.

Sadhana: telling a family story

To help children learn about the genre of storywriting, Sadhana's teacher asked her pupils to write a story starting from an everyday situation such as going shopping, and make it exciting by introducing an unexpected event. When Sadhana was asked what she was going to write about, she replied 'going to the park', and the exciting thing which happened would be 'I saw my Nanny'. For Sadhana, this would indeed be an unusual event because her grandmother lived in Ecuador.

Sadhana was very close to her grandmother despite the distance separating them. They talked on the phone, and visited each other in London or Ecuador about every six months. The idea of writing about her grandmother was particularly motivating for Sadhana, and she began to write as soon as she was given her class exercise book.

Although Sadhana was not always a fast writer, on this occasion she wrote quite rapidly, saying the words as she went along and sounding some of them out in a whisper. She also read back to herself what she had written, sometimes pausing for further thought. After writing several lines she stopped, smiled, picked up her book and took it to show her teacher.

This was how Sadhana read out her story (see Figure 20):

> On the morning I went to the park I saw my granny. My granny gave me a present. I love my granny ... my granny she was happy and I went to Tesco. We buyed some rice and Cornflakes, then I went to

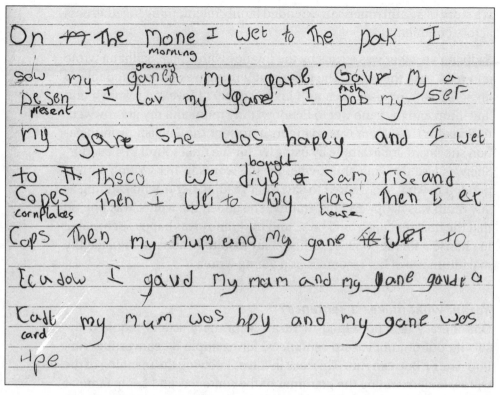

On ~~the~~ The Mone [morning] I wet to The park I

sow my ganeñ [granny] my gane Gàvr my a

pesen [present] I lav my gane I [mish] pob my ser

my gare She wos hapey and I wet

to ~~th~~ Thsco We diyb [bought] ¢ sam rise and

Copes [Cornflakes] Then I Wri to my [house] plas Then I er

Cops Then my mum and my gane ~~te~~ WeT to

Ecudow I gavd my mam and my gane gavdr a

Cadt [card] my mum wos hpy and my gane wos

Hpe

Figure 20: Sadhana's story about going to the park and meeting her grandmother from Ecuador.

my house, then I ate Cornflakes. Then my mum and my granny went to Ecuador. I gave my mum and my granny gave a card. My mum was happy and my granny.

This is a complete story with a beginning and a happy ending. In between there are a number of key events. Sadhana's description of going to the supermarket and choosing her favourite food, closely followed by the departure of her mother and grandmother to a destination thousands of miles away, seems a combination of the everyday and the dramatic. However, Sadhana's life involved a good deal of family travel to and from Ecuador, so this was a perfectly possible sequence of events, each of which had special significance to her.

I later discovered that Sadhana's mother was actually in Ecuador at the time Sadhana was writing. In the story, the importance of her relationship with her mother and grandmother is expressed through the exchange of cards, and the result of Sadhana's story is family happiness. It is a story of a Latin American extended family maintaining togetherness across continents.

Sadhana's teacher was struck by the fluency with which Sadhana wrote and read back this story. The emergent writing was understandable to an adult, with phrases such as 'I lav my gane' ('I love my granny') and 'my mum and my gane wet to Ecudow' ('my mum and my granny went to Ecuador'). Sadhana was trying to represent the English pronunciation she heard, for example by using 'w' for the final sound in 'Ecuador'. She was also thinking about whether the words in her writing corresponded to what she wanted to say. After reading her original ending as 'my mum was happy and my granny', she added the words 'was hpe' so that the final reading would be '... and my granny was happy'. Being able to choose a theme so close to her heart inspired Sadhana to make the maximum use of her resources as a young writer.

Yazan: what makes a sentence?

One literacy task presented to Yazan in primary school required the sorting out of jumbled-up sentences, for example by converting 'run. Bob can' to 'Bob can run.' This task involves knowing the meaning of the words, understanding the grammar of the sentence, and being familiar with the rules of punctuation. None of these aspects is straightforward, particularly for a second language learner. Yazan had only arrived in England two years earlier, so English was still new to him in many ways.

Figure 21 shows how Yazan completed the task, and this is how he tackled each part. Yazan's first priority was to try to make sense of the phrases. He was quite satisfied when he produced 'can Bob run' for the first sentence. Punctuation took a secondary place for Yazan at this time, so having found a version which was meaningful he paid no attention to the full stop after the word 'run' on the worksheet. The next sentence, 'cat The fat. is' quickly became 'The cat is fat' and Yazan was also confident in changing 'A hid. fox' to 'A fox hid'. In neither case did he use the full stop; this was not his main focus.

But when he reached 'Sam wet? Did get' he commented 'This one is hard'. He tried out several combinations, first reading 'Sam' as 'Sem' and then deciding it was 'Sam'. Although the vocabulary had been chosen to be simple and easy to read, with only two- or three-letter words, English names like Sam were not necessarily familiar to Yazan. He also seemed unsure about the word 'Did', first trying 'dog', then 'dit', and finally 'did',

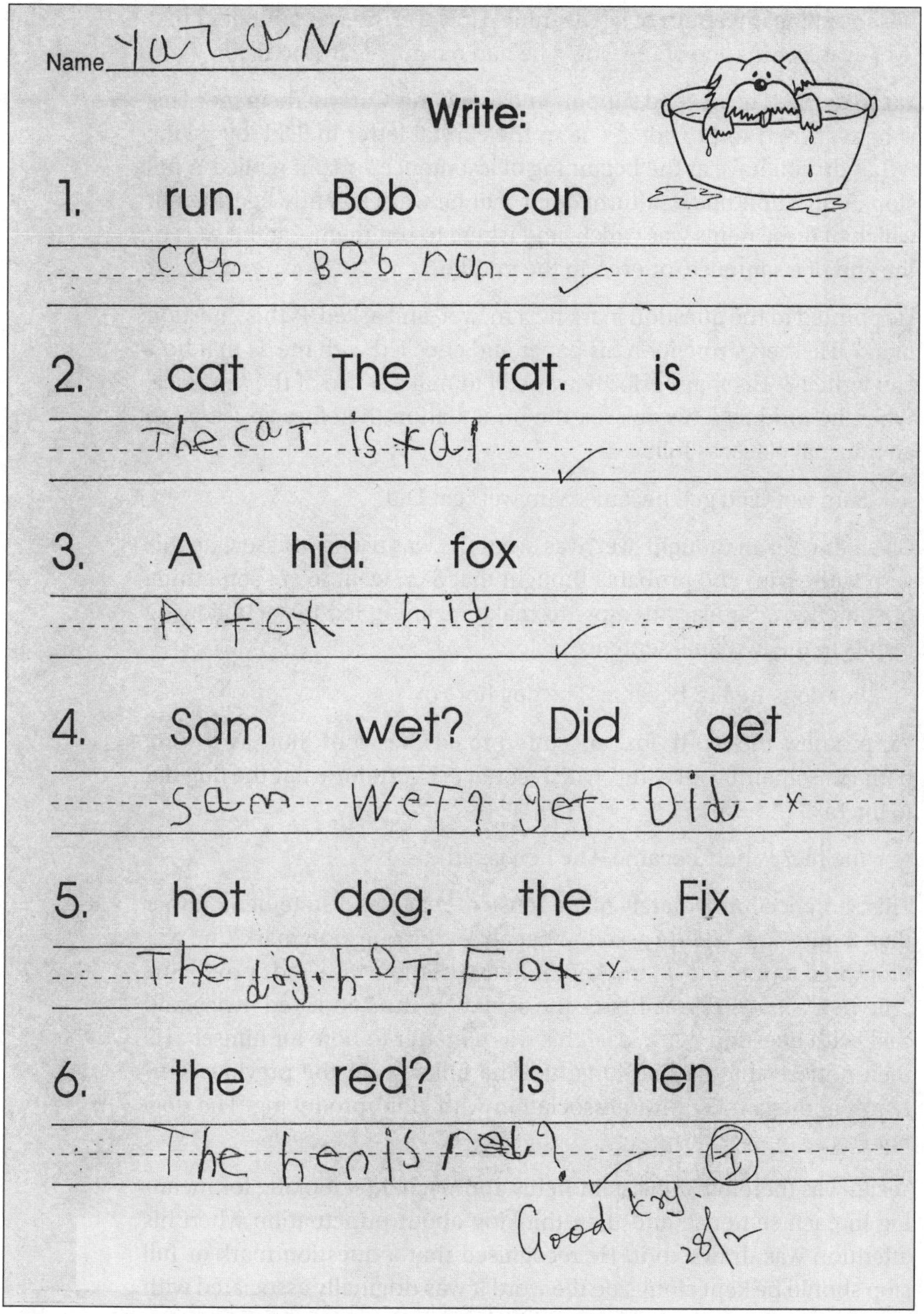

Name _YaZaN_

Write:

1. run.   Bob   can

    CAp BOb rUn ✓

2. cat   The   fat.   is

    The caT is fal ✓

3. A   hid.   fox

    A fox   hid ✓

4. Sam   wet?   Did   get

    Sam WeT? get Did ✗

5. hot   dog.   the   Fix

    The dog. hOT Fox ✗

6. the   red?   Is   hen

    The hen is red? ✓   ①

    Good try.
    28/₂

Figure 21: Yazan's solution to the jumbled sentences task.

but sounding uncertain of its meaning. However, he was confident that 'wet' was 'went' (one of the words he had recently learnt to read).

Yazan decided he needed support and asked me 'Can you help me? This is hard'. I tried to provide a cue to the capital letter in 'Did' by asking 'What do you have at the beginning of a sentence?' Yazan replied 'A full stop. A question mark'. It turned out that he was currently figuring out which of these items was which, and where to put them – at the start or the end of a sentence, or even in the middle?

He pointed to the question mark next to 'wet' and asked 'Is this question mark?' He then wrote it on his paper and checked with me 'Is that how you write it?' His main priority was still to make sense of the sentence. When he produced his answer, the punctuation therefore appeared in an unusual place, as follows:

'Sam wet? Did get' became 'Sam wet? get Did'

Given that Yazan thought 'wet' was 'went', he was trying to associate this verb with 'Sam', and probably thought that Sam went to get something or somebody. Similar attempts to make meaning led to the following results in the two final sentences:

'hot dog. the Fix' became 'The dog hot Fox'

Yazan knew the word 'fox' and interpreted the word 'hot' as a verb, perhaps something like 'hit', which could account for what the dog did to the fox.

'the red? Is hen' became 'The hen is red'

This sentence immediately made sense to Yazan as a statement, rather than a question. When I asked 'What about the question mark?', he was prompted to include it, and kept it in association with 'red', producing 'The hen is red?' He read back the sentence 'the hen is red' twice and said 'with question mark', as if this was a matter to note for himself. He then noticed that he had forgotten the full stop in the previous sentence, and again kept it in association with 'dog', producing 'The dog. hot Fox'.

Yazan was therefore consistent in his approach, first looking for meaning in each sentence and then thinking about punctuation when his attention was drawn to it. He recognised that a question mark or full stop should be kept alongside the word it was originally associated with on the worksheet. Capital letters, which might have been a clue to the start of the sentence, were not Yazan's focus – possibly because they are not an infallible guide, since they are also used for proper names.

The approach taken by Yazan was validated by his teacher's response, which suggests that he knew what counted as important in this classroom. She allowed his sentences as correct if they made sense, even if the punctuation was missing or incorrectly placed. The only sentences which she marked wrong were 'Sam wet? get Did' and 'The dog. hot Fox'. She had not heard Yazan sounding out these words, as I had, and therefore it was difficult for her to see how he had made meaning from them. She agreed, however, that 'Fix the hot dog' was difficult to interpret, since it was not a common phrase in English.

Throughout this exercise, Yazan applied the knowledge he currently had to the task. He showed his emerging awareness of punctuation, a tricky concept which can take a while for children to figure out. Three months later, when I observed him again, Yazan had clarified for himself that sentences must begin with a capital letter and end with a question mark or full stop.

Tala: exploring long vowels

In Tala's class, each child had drawn a picture of their own face and was now writing a description to accompany the drawing. Tala was involved in spelling out the words 'eyes' and 'mouth', for which she suggested 'E-A-I-S' and 'M-O-A-F'. Although the vowels she chose were not quite correct, she had noticed that these were long vowel sounds. She therefore used two or three letters to represent them in each case.

Tala employed the same principle for the following words: 'tooth' became 'tuaiec', 'hair' became 'haer', and 'face' became 'faes'. She began trying these words out in statements about herself. Saying 'I love writing', she wrote rapidly on the back of her picture:

my eais r blue	(my eyes are blue)
my ears r piesh	(my ears are peach)
my hand r peaink	(my hands are pink)
my nos r piesh	(my nose are peach)

Tala's writing contained a variety of approaches to spelling. There were several words which she knew how to spell conventionally, some quite challenging, such as 'ears' and 'blue'. The letter-name 'R' is often used by children to stand for 'are', and it is possible that Tala had also seen this as a convention in mobile phone text-messaging. But what stands out is the use of more than one vowel to represent long vowel sounds.

Tala's teacher commented that she was a confident writer who was able to express herself on paper. For example, she would write at length in her Monday 'news book' about her experiences at the weekend. Her writing was always readable to an adult who was familiar with her current style. Tala knew the alphabet and letter-sound links and could write some consonant blends such as 'sh'. In fact, she was particularly keen on using 'sh' at present, and on exploring how to write long vowel sounds.

In the examples above, Tala's current interest even overflowed into the word 'pink', which acquired multiple vowels. Her ears and nose could easily have been described as 'pink' as well, but the word 'peach' gave her the chance to become more poetic, as well as drawing on her interest in long vowel sounds and her simultaneous fondness for using 'sh'. Here we can see the enjoyment of a child who is experimenting simultaneously with spelling and self-expression.

Ming: writing nursery rhymes

Ming and his classmates read aloud the book *Rhymes to Remember* with the help of their teacher, doing actions along with their reading. Afterwards, children were given the first line of several nursery rhymes, and they had to write the second line in each case. Ming's response to this task is shown in Figure 22.

The first example was 'Jack and Jill', for which the continuation should be 'went up the hill'. Ming wrote down 'jack and jill' and said 'went on the hill'. He confidently wrote 'went on the' and then asked 'how do you spell hill?' Seeing that he would have to decide for himself, he wrote 'hil' and then commented 'I need another letter' and added 'e' to make 'hile'. It is likely that 'hil' looked wrong to him, and that the idea of adding another letter reminded him of the strategy of adding 'e' at the end of some words (the so-called 'magic E' which has the effect of lengthening the central vowel sound). The 'magic E' is not needed here, but Ming was searching through his current resources to solve the problem.

For the second rhyme, beginning 'Hickory Dickory Dock', the next line should be 'the mouse ran up the clock'. Ming quickly wrote 'the mouse'. Laughing, he told me 'I copied that up there – it's on the wall!' Indeed, the word 'mouse' appeared in the classroom alphabet chart. Ming

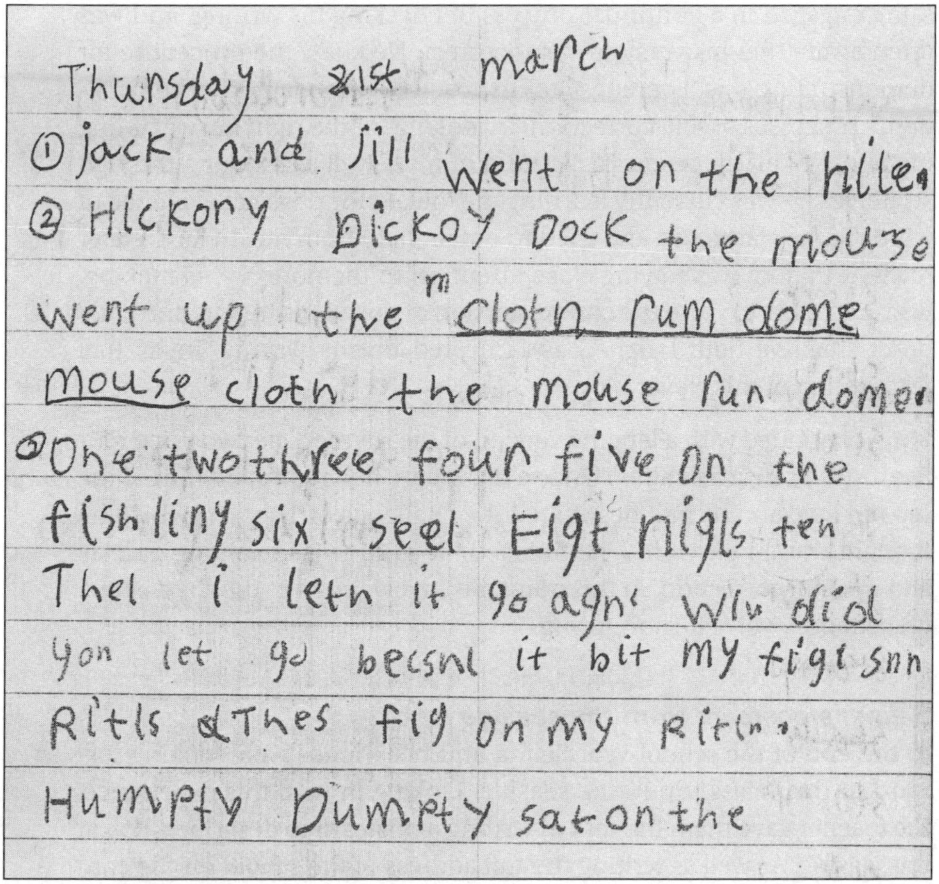

Thursday 31st march

① jack and Jill went on the hile.

② Hickory Dickoy Dock the mouse

went up the ᵐclotn rum dome

mouse cloth the mouse run dome.

③ One two three four five on the

fish liny six seel Eigt nigls ten

Thel i letn it go agni wlu did

you let go becsnl it bit my figt snn

Ritls dThes fig on my ritn.

Humpty Dumpty sat on the

Figure 22: Ming writing nursery rhymes.

followed this by writing 'went up the' and said 'clock'. He began with 'c' and sounded out 'c-l', writing 'clo' as a result.

On saying the word 'clock' again, Ming used the London pronunciation which makes the final sound into a glottal stop. This presented him with something of a challenge when trying to finish the written word. He tried 't' as an ending, looked again and added 'n', making 'clotn'. He repeated the word out loud, 'clock'.

The next line would be 'the mouse ran down'. Saying 'ran down', Ming wrote 'rum dome'. But he realised that he had left out 'the mouse' and said 'I done it wrong', underlining 'clotn rum dome' and explaining to me 'you have to underline it if you do a mistake'. Finally, he re-wrote 'clotn', added 'the mouse run dome' and was satisfied. Both his rhymes ended with a prominent full stop.

Ming engaged in a continual process of checking his writing, and was often aware that his version was incorrect. He knew the procedure for demonstrating this awareness to his teacher, who wanted to see children's processes of self-correction. In looking for the right answer, Ming made use of all the resources around him. As well as thinking through strategies he was currently learning, he looked for physical evidence of words in the classroom and tried to obtain help from me. In fact, I later realised that he was paying close attention to the notes I was making, waiting for me to write the correct version of the words he was currently producing! We both laughed as I covered up my writing, in mutual recognition of this clever ploy.

Ming continued with a lengthy version of the rhyme 'One two three four five, once I saw a fish alive'. Once a classmate had reminded him of the second line, and he had negotiated the challenge of 'fishali' – which he thought was a new word – he finished the entire verse, writing quickly and without correction. At this point, his involvement in the rhyme took precedence over self-monitoring.

Selina: a postcard from the seaside
At the end of the school year Selina and her friends were looking forward to their class trip to the seaside. Linking in with this experience, the teacher gave them the task of writing a postcard to describe a day at the seaside. As well as writing the full address of the school on the card as requested, Selina added her mother's name above.

When she had spent some time rubbing out various versions and receiving advice from her teacher, Selina's postcard read:

Dear mum,

I went to the sea-side it was so hot. So I went to the sea to cool down then I stand upand and dryed my self but I was cold so I Ran about and had fun. I was hurrug so I ate my lunch and I mada a sand castle. when I kept on digging then I saw a crab so I stoped making my sand castle and played with my crab and then we picked up shell and played water agin.

Love

from:

Selina

Here Selina uses conjunctions such as 'so', 'then' and 'but' with considerable style. She has incorporated the key vocabulary offered by her teacher into a sequence of events which makes a coherent narrative. Some of the words involved were still in the process of settling in her mind – for example, when she was re-writing the postcard with final corrections from her teacher, she began the word 'kept' with a 'c' but immediately altered it to 'k'. Her use of capital letters was well-developed, with the occasional variation such as 'Ran' in the middle of a sentence, and she gave her sentences prominent full stops.

The final version of Selina's postcard (Figure 23) used the same material, this time addressed to her friend Thalia, and decorated with a border of seaside motifs: buckets and spades, starfish, sandcastles, fish and ice-cream. Selina and her friend Ruby spent a long time working on their borders together, designing the motifs and choosing colours. Selina's sandcastles shared features with Ruby's islands, having trees sprouting out of them as well as flags. She also retained the elegant version of the letter 'f' in 'from Selina', her characteristic way of writing the word 'from' in letters and cards at the time. Satisfied with their creations, Selina and Ruby left for morning assembly hand-in-hand.

The need to extend bilingual learning

All the children in the project made progress in both their literacies during the year. With regard to English, Yazan and Sadhana were receiving extra support in primary school. The other children were not considered to need such support because they had been born in Britain and often spoke English with older siblings. As the examples above show, each child approached their learning of English with a good deal of thought, figuring out the principles involved.

With regard to Chinese, Arabic or Spanish, the children had less opportunity to study than in English – just a few hours a week. This is 'learning at the margins', only possible because of the dedicated support of their families and voluntary-run community schools. Despite the difficult circumstances under which children were learning their community language, they were still able to begin writing in that script. As they did so, they gained insights into how the writing system worked in comparison to English. This shows the potential gains from becoming bi-literate, and emphasises the need to properly support and fund community language schools.

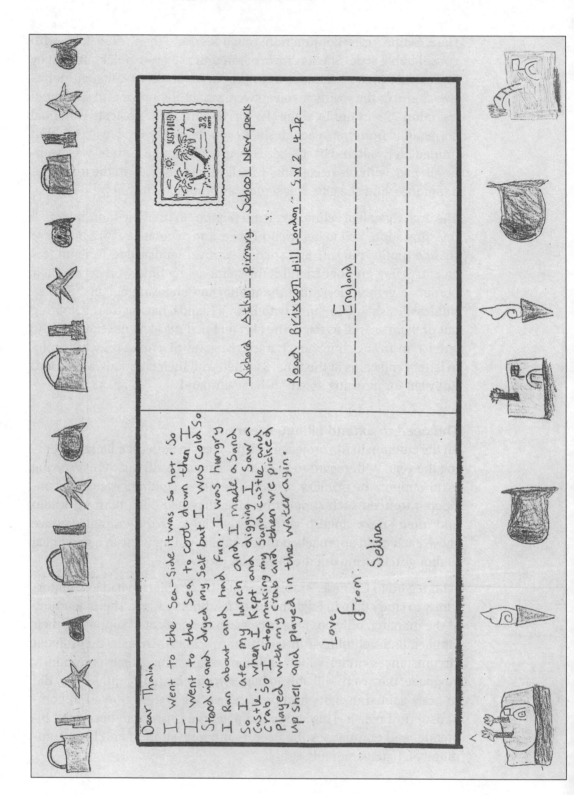

Dear Thalia

I went to the sea-side it was so hot. So I went to the sea to cool down then I Stood up and dryed my self but I was cold So I Ran about and had Fun. I was hungry So I ate my lunch and I made a Sand Castle. when I Kept and digging I saw a crab so I Stop making my Sand castle and Played with my crab and then we picked up shell and played in the water ajin.

Love
from.
Selina

Richard ___ Atkm ___ pirimary ___ School New pork

Road__Brixton hill London -- 5 w 2 4 jp

England

The children's classmates also relished the chance to learn about different scripts. Their positive response points to the benefits which could result from teaching languages in the early years of schooling – an approach which could involve both bilingual and monolingual children.

Ideas for promoting language learning in school

■ If you know that a child is learning another literacy, you can ask them to show you how they write in that language. You could then ask what is similar or different to English. This will help to gain insight into their current thinking on how writing works.

■ When observing a bilingual child doing a writing task in the classroom, you are likely to see them using some of the strategies mentioned in this chapter: trying to find the best way to represent sounds in English (and perhaps comparing them to similar sounds or letters in another language); working on an issue such as directionality (trying out alternatives); figuring out how punctuation works; prioritising an issue such as how to represent long vowel sounds. Each child will have an individual approach and, as their teacher, you will be able to identify this and help them think their ideas through.

■ Your school could extend its language learning curriculum by investigating opportunities for teaching languages already spoken by some pupils. Chinese, Arabic and Spanish are official languages of the United Nations and are widely used in the world. Other languages are equally important and valuable, giving access to literature and cultural experience, work opportunities in locations ranging from hospitals to airports, and business and trade with different countries. Plus if children learn a language spoken by classmates, they have a ready-made reason to communicate. In England, the National Languages Strategy is opening up possibilities for different languages to be taught at primary level.

■ If a language is being taught at primary school, children who speak that language or study it at Saturday school can help their peers to learn, as shown by the peer teaching sessions in this research project. Special classes can also be arranged for native

opposite: *Figure 23: The final version of Selina's seaside postcard.*

speakers, to support their own language and literacy development.

■ You can build a multilingual learning environment in your classroom by inviting parents, grandparents or siblings to demonstrate activities such as cooking, crafts or storytelling in different languages. This puts them in the 'expert' role and raises the status of child and family within the school. Literacy activities could range from designing film posters to writing stories or making newspapers. Examples are given in my book *Home Pages* (2000).

■ Materials in a range of different languages can be used to raise language awareness. Such awareness prepares children to learn languages now or in the future. It also encourages them to think about the distinctive features of the English writing system. *Curriculum Guidance for the Foundation Stage* (QCA, 2000:44) requires practitioners to plan 'opportunities for children to become aware of languages and writing systems other than English', and states that 'children's experience of different scripts at home should be acknowledged and built on when learning about the conventions of English' (*ibid*: 47).

■ You can take a language awareness approach when working on any aspect of literacy, asking bilingual children to compare English with other languages they know and share their ideas with classmates who are unfamiliar with them. For example, how does that language deal with adjectives, verb endings, plurals, or word order?

■ Using materials ranging from food wrappers to newspapers and storybooks you can ask children:

- What type of text do you think this is?

- How do you know even if you can't read the words? (this draws attention to the uses of layout, images, design and fonts)

- What do you think it says? (this encourages children to use reading strategies such as prediction)

- If the text is in English and another language, even if you don't know the other script, can you match up words and phrases between the two languages? What might they mean in the other language? Does the other language use punctuation or capital letters in the same way as English?

Children enjoy 'cracking the code' and puzzling out the new system by comparing it to English – it's a challenge, often more motivating than studying English alone.

■ For links to websites on multilingual resources for children, see the National Literacy Trust site: www.literacytrust.org.uk/database/EALres.html

3

Writing different scripts

't's wonky and it's not straight' was Ming's verdict on a primary school classmate's attempt to write a Chinese character. Tala made a similarly observant comment when teaching her friend Bhumi to write a word in Arabic: 'You forgot to do that little wiggly line'. Why were the children so concerned about the exact form of their classmates' writing? It turned out that Ming and Tala were interpreting their Saturday school teachers' instructions on how to write symbols in Chinese or Arabic. The children had worked out that certain criteria were significant when writing a character, a letter or a word. If these criteria were not followed the writing would 'look wrong', resulting in a change in meaning.

Young children divine that meaning does not only reside in the writing of a whole sentence or even a whole word. It also resides in the writing of a single letter, or a mark such as an accent or a full stop. Equally important may be the placing of writing on the page; does the page operate with horizontal lines or with vertical columns, and in which direction does the writing go?

Children becoming biliterate find out that different scripts operate by different rules. Even scripts which look similar have their special attributes. As Brian remarked when comparing English to Spanish, 'They haven't got a N with *this* on top' (referring to the letter 'ñ' as in 'España').

Biliterate children widen their horizons with respect to the making and placing of marks on the page. They have to recognise what counts as important in each script and be able to produce their own version, whether this involves writing from left to right in Arabic and right to left in English, or using Chinese stroke patterns as compared to English 'joined-up writing'. The children in our research project were developing an impressive range of visual and actional capabilities, due to their experience of different scripts.

The act of writing

Handwriting has often been thought of as a purely mechanical skill. Yet the act of writing is cultural, involving both body and mind. Rosemary Sassoon, who has investigated the writing of different scripts, says that: 'To write we use our whole selves, our minds and our bodies. Our mark is a personal one, indicative of our character, our training and our culture' (1995: 7). We even have a saying 'to make your mark', which originates from the impact of being able to produce a graphic sign that identified you personally. Young children often go to great lengths to design symbols which are particular to them, such as the curly 'f' Selina always included when signing her name 'from Selina'.

At the same time, as Sassoon points out, the way an individual writes is shaped by their learning environment. She therefore suggests that: 'In acquiring a second writing system you may be acquiring another cultural philosophy; you certainly are acquiring another set of physical movements and maybe with it a different way of thinking altogether' (1995: 7).

The act of writing is recognised in some countries as an important part of the literacy curriculum. In France, for example, the teaching of handwriting is underpinned by a holistic philosophy called *le graphisme* (Thomas, 1997). The nearest English translation would be 'the graphic act', and according to this approach handwriting is *un act complexe* (a complex action) involving *un geste delicat* (a delicate movement).

The aim of *le graphisme* is to develop children's visual and bodily awareness through a variety of activities, in art and physical education as well as in actions using pen and pencil. Four-year-olds focus on particular aspects of works of art, such as pointillism in Seurat or lines in Picasso, and then design their own patterns. In physical education, children practise wavy movements with their whole body and make patterns with streamers in the air, before learning a new handwriting pattern involving a wavy motion.

This approach is seen as preparation for the understanding and production of writing. Children will eventually be able to create their own cursive script, which is considered fundamental to becoming a culturally competent writer. Similar ideas can be found in the British book *The Dance of the Pen* by Paul Ansell, Gaynor Kitchener and Sally Potter (1994). The authors conceptualise writing as a 'rhythmical pattern making activity' and recommend that children should work large-scale in paint, crayon or chalk. As well as linking writing with the visual mode, they also connect it to the mode of sound, suggesting that children can form the patterns while listening to music with a strong rhythm. Through such activities, children will gain the pleasure of developing their particular handwriting style.

Multimodal learning

The philosophy of *le graphisme* draws our attention to the visual and kinaesthetic aspects of learning to write. These are intimately linked with the cognitive understanding of writing, according to Gunther Kress (1997, 2000). He argues that learning to produce and interpret written graphic symbols is a multimodal experience. As children write, they make use of various modes including those of the visual and of action to think about how writing makes meaning. Whether writing with pen on paper or cutting out shapes with scissors, 'children act multimodally, both in the things they use, the objects they make, and in the engagement of their bodies; there is no separation of body and mind' (1997: 97).

Kress explains that all modes of representation offer different potentials and limitations. Each writing system uses the visual and actional modes in particular ways. When children produce written symbols they have to pay attention to a number of different facets – the type of stroke to be used, directionality, shape, size, spatial orientation, placement on the page – and these will be culturally specified in the teaching experienced by the child.

From these features, children create their own repertoire of representational resources. Children learning different writing systems through culturally different pedagogies will expand their multisemiotic resources (Kenner and Kress, 2003), an advantage in today's world of international multimodal communication. Making use of different modes 'offers an enormous potential enrichment, cognitively, conceptually, aesthetically and affectively' (Kress, 1997: 29).

In the previous chapter we saw how children have individual pathways of learning as they find out about the alphabetic or the logographic principle, for example. In a similar way, each child forms particular interpretations of what is important in the act of writing. Tala, Yazan, Sadhana, Brian, Selina and Ming observed the input of their teachers, parents and siblings on how to write in Arabic, Spanish or Chinese as well as English. From this, they made decisions about how symbols are created and positioned in each writing system.

Three main issues seemed significant to the children: how symbols were designed, the spatial location of writing on the page, and directionality. Here I shall explain how each writing system deals with these issues and how the children perceived them.

The design of symbols
The precision of Chinese characters

Each Chinese character has to be written with careful attention to detail, because a small difference in the stroke pattern can make it look like another character with a different meaning. So as soon as they begin to learn about writing, children need to practise the basic stroke types which are the building blocks of the writing system. The individual strokes are of particular lengths and placed at particular angles, and some are straight whilst others are curved.

Next, children learn sequences of strokes which make up particular characters. The sequence has a certain order, to make sure the pattern is built up correctly and the result looks harmonious. The aesthetic appearance of the character is considered very important.

To memorise the stroke sequence, children practise each character many times. The whole process is shown in a page from Selina's first year exercise book at Chinese school, when she was five years old (Figure 24). In the right hand column, Selina has written the complete sequence to produce the character 'younger sister'. Once the character is complete, she has practised it in six more columns moving from right to left across the page.

In English primary school, children are not expected to show such pen control at the age of five. However, this capability is necessary in order to write in Chinese. Children also need to be able to recognise small differences in stroke patterns, to check that they have written each character correctly. Selina, Ming and their classmates at Chinese school

Figure 24: From Selina's first-year exercise book at Chinese school: learning the stroke sequence to build up a character (in the right hand column) and practising the whole character.

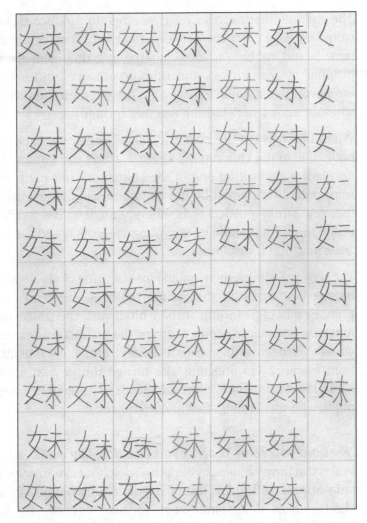

were developing their visual and actional capacities through close attention and continual practice, so that they could produce these complex patterns.

They were helped by their teachers, who would write similar-looking stroke patterns on the board and ask children to spot the difference. Children would volunteer that 'it's too straight' (when the stroke should be curved) or 'it's too far away' (when two strokes should be placed closer together). The teacher would remind them to be precise when writing each stroke, saying for example 'Make sure it's only like a little one – a short line'. As teacher and pupils discussed the stroke pattern together, children built up a vocabulary for concepts of shape, angle and size in both English and Cantonese.

The children themselves were concerned to produce characters which were beautifully written as well as correct. They brought an array of pencils and rubbers to class, sharpening their pencils frequently to produce clearer strokes, and rubbing out over and over again. They often compared their efforts to those of their friends and decided whether each other's writing was well formed.

When I first visited the class and was sitting at the back with my notebook, one of the children asked me 'Haven't you got anything to do?' I decided to try writing one of the characters and my beginner efforts were politely corrected by the children sitting near me. It turned out that one stroke needed to be sharply angled 'like a tick' rather than rounded, as I had done it. My young mentors could see the difference and knew that it was important.

The sense of achievement gained from writing characters could be seen on the first occasion that Selina taught Chinese to a classmate at primary school. Standing at the whiteboard, she proceeded to write a nineteen-step sequence to produce the character meaning 'read'. Her strokes were powerful and well-defined, and she wrote almost entirely from memory. On finishing, she turned round with a smile of satisfaction and came back to the table with a spring in her step to help her pupil, who was both baffled and impressed.

'Pretend you're in Year 1...you can do easy ones'

When teaching Chinese to her primary school classmates, Selina took a strict approach. The first time she taught Ruby, her best friend at school, she began by demonstrating the stroke sequence for the character meaning 'tomorrow'. This was an eight-step sequence and Selina expected Ruby to be able to reproduce it correctly. Ruby was keen to learn, but found the task a challenge. The only verbal instructions she received from Selina were 'do it like this one' (i.e. follow the model) and 'don't do it big'.

Finding that Ruby needed help, Selina completed the stroke sequence for her and then told her to 'do three' (meaning that she should practise the whole character for three columns). With considerable effort, Ruby completed one column. Selina inspected her pupil's work and found it fell below her high standards. To Ruby's dismay, she rubbed out the entire column and showed her the sequence again.

Once again, Selina gave little verbal feedback, expecting Ruby to identify her mistakes and and correct them by carefully studying the visual details of the example. Gradually she realised that Ruby was unaccustomed to such an approach and needed explicit comments to draw her attention to key criteria, such as 'not like a square' when the stroke pattern was rectangular. Selina therefore decided to simplify the content of the lesson.

She told her friend 'Pretend you're in Year 1 in Chinese school ... you can do easy ones' (Selina herself was then in Year 2 in Chinese school). She selected a character which contained fewer strokes, but some of them were curved. Ruby had difficulty with these, as she had earlier with the curved stroke in 'tomorrow', which she had written as a straight line. Either she perceived the subtle curve as straight, or she found the angle and sweep of the curve hard to reproduce.

This event emphasises the capacities Selina had built up from learning Chinese. Ruby quickly realised that precision was important and that she had to continually make visual comparisons between her writing and Selina's example. She began to critique her own work with comments such as 'That bit was too long'. However, it was difficult for Ruby to notice such small differences and to write strokes with such accuracy, because she had not experienced this teaching before. Her lessons with Selina offered her opportunities to extend her visual and actional abilities.

Selina's response to Ruby showed that each small detail of the characters held significance for her. The meaning of the character lay not only in what it stood for, but also in the precision of the strokes and the relationship of one stroke to another. Selina was particularly concerned with the detail of Chinese writing because her mother emphasised this in their evening lessons together. Susannah, her older sister, also gave advice to Selina when teaching her to write characters in preparation for the following Saturday's class.

Key differences in stroke patterns

Ming's family did not put so much emphasis on teaching stroke production, and Ming was less concerned with complete accuracy when teaching his classmates at primary school. However, he showed that he was aware of criteria such as the correct length, angle and balance of strokes when he made comments such as 'Make it even more bigger' or

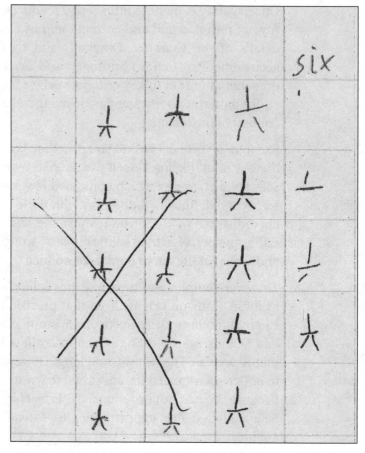

Figure 25: Ming put a cross through Roberto's writing of the Chinese character for 'six' because he considered the vertical line to be 'too long' at certain points, and the strokes underneath the horizontal line to be too close together.

criticised his own writing by saying 'That's too lumpy'. He decided to do a circle round one offending character 'cos that's what my Chinese teacher does when I get it wrong'.

Ming also knew that small variations in stroke pattern could differentiate between two potentially similar characters. When teaching his classmate Roberto to write the character meaning 'six' (Figure 25), Ming suddenly became dissatisfied with his pupil's efforts. He complained that at some points Roberto's writing of the upper vertical stroke was 'too long', and that the lower part of the character was wrong 'because it's next to each other' (the two strokes under the horizontal line were supposed to be further apart). It turned out that these details were indeed significant in differentiating this character from the one meaning 'big'(Figure 26).

Figure 26: The Chinese characters for 'six' (on the left) and 'big' (on right).

Understanding the sequence

Although he was not yet confident about writing many characters, Ming understood the concept of writing strokes in a certain order. He devised a 'test' for Roberto, drawing a horizontal grid which his pupil was to use to demonstrate the stroke sequence for the character 'six' (Figure 27).

Just as in the tests Ming did at Chinese school, the whole character was written in the left-hand box by the 'teacher' and Roberto was expected to build up each step of the stroke sequence in the rest of the grid. Finding that his friend was somewhat baffled, Ming sought to help by completing the grid himself.

Figure 27: Ming's grid to test knowledge of the stroke sequence for the character 'six'.

I watched Ming produce more grids of this kind when he was preparing a Chinese test for his whole primary school class. Sometimes when he came to check the grid he found he had included slightly too many boxes, or too few. However, it was striking that he was able to make an approximate judgement about the number of boxes required without actually writing the stroke sequence down first. This showed that he had a sense of how many steps were involved in a particular pattern – a highly developed visual technique.

Joined letter forms in Arabic

Arabic, like English and Spanish, is an alphabetic system, so symbols do not have to be written quite as accurately as in Chinese. Instead of having thousands of characters that are subtly different from one another, alphabetic scripts have a defined set of letters which can be more easily distinguished. Readers usually encounter letters in the context of a word, giving further clues as to what the letter might be.

However, in Arabic a number of concerns still arise for learners about certain details of each letter, because the letters take different forms when they are at the beginning, in the middle or at the end of a word. Children have to know how to produce each shape and how to join it to others. They also need to guard against letters looking too similar to each other when joined.

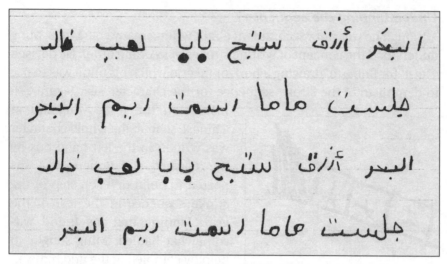

Figure 28: Tala's writing in her Arabic school exercise book.

At Arabic school, teachers helped children to develop their abilities for visual discrimination by writing words on the board and asking which letters they were composed of. They also requested children themselves to write words on the board so that the whole class could decide if the letters had been correctly formed and joined. If children needed help to remember these characteristics and to write the script appropriately, teachers provided support through a join-the-dots model of a word on the board or in exercise books. This was an aid both to perception and action.

Lines from Tala's exercise book that she wrote at age six demonstrate the joined-up nature of Arabic writing (Figure 28). By this point Tala was already proficient in using joined letter forms, and she knew which letters could not join to the left (as mentioned in Chapter 2, there are six of these 'stubborn' letters). I shall now describe a peer teaching event led by Tala, in which she demonstrated her concern about the correct way to write a certain letter.

'You forgot to do that little wiggly line'

Tala decided to teach the word 'mama' (mum) to her friends Tina and Bhumi. Just like her teachers in Arabic school, she provided a join the dots version to help her pupils to write the word. She then decided to write over the dots herself, giving them a model to follow (Figure 29). One of the original dots can still be seen in the loop of the first syllable.

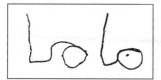

Figure 29: Tala's writing of the Arabic word 'mama' (mum). The symbol on the left shows a pronounced 'wiggle'.

Writing the word 'mama' in Arabic involves joining the letter 'mim' (for the sound 'm') to the letter 'alif' (for the sound 'a'), twice over. First you have to write the initial form of 'mim', and join it to the middle form of 'alif', making 'ma'. Since 'alif' is one of the 'stubborn' letters which cannot join to the left, you then have to leave a gap before starting the next syllable. The second syllable is identical to the first.

When Tina began writing the word, using the model provided, Tala shrieked and grabbed the sheet of paper from her, saying 'Tina, you ain't doing the stick so good – do the circle here and then you do the line'. Tracing the letters with her finger, she emphasised the necessary action for connecting the 'circle' of 'mim' to the 'stick' of 'alif'.

Tina began again, but Tala was still dissatisfied. She said 'you got to do the line, there', tracing the shape with her finger once more, and rubbing out Tina's new version. The 'line' at issue seemed to be the wiggle which follows the loop of 'mim' as it joins to the vertical stroke of 'alif' – this is clearly visible in the left-hand part of Figure 29. This time Tala gave Tina more precise instructions: 'you're doing a circle, right, but you always forget to do the line', while demonstrating writing a circle followed by a pronounced wiggle. Tina understood, and responded by including a wiggle in her next version. Later Tala explained to her other pupil Bhumi, who was trying to write the same word, 'you done it wrong because you forgot to do that little wiggly line'.

Why was Tala so concerned about the wiggle? It turns out that when joining 'mim' to 'alif', the horizontal line following the circle is needed to differentiate this form of 'mim' from another letter, 'waw'. Making the horizontal line more pronounced, as a wiggle, clarifies the distinction further, ensuring that 'mim' is not read as 'waw'. Tala was aware of this subtle distinction and did not consider the word to be correct without it.

Just as Selina and Ming focused on specific details of Chinese characters which they considered to alter the meaning, so Tala picked out the 'wiggle' as the key attribute when linking these two particular letters. This is a complex task for children; out of all the instruction they receive on the act of writing, they have to identify what really matters when distinguishing one letter or character from another. Teachers at Chinese and Arabic school helped children to understand significant details of this kind by emphasising them in discussion.

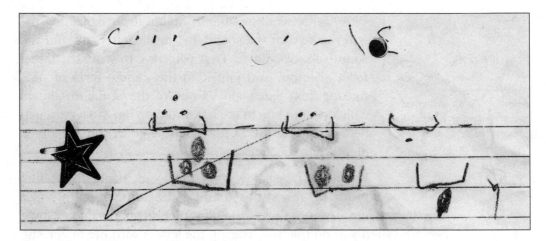

Figure 30: In Yazan's writing of the first few letters of the Arabic alphabet he used much bigger dots than in the examples provided by his teacher, showing that he knew the dots were important.

For Tala, as for Ming and Selina, the meaning of each word resided both in knowing what it stood for and how it should be written. In a later peer teaching session, when other 'pupils' had produced the written form of 'mama' to her satisfaction, she commented 'That means you know it'.

The importance of dots in Arabic

Dots are a significant feature in Arabic writing because they distinguish otherwise similar-looking letters from each other. For example, the letters 'ba', 'ta' and 'tha' all have an upturned half-moon shape, but 'ba' has one dot underneath, 'ta' has two dots above and 'tha' has three dots above. Figure 30 shows Yazan practising the three letters, following an example given by his teacher.

Teachers and family members would encourage children to 'remember the dots' when writing, and Yazan had certainly taken note of this message. His writing shows a particular focus on the dots – in fact, they have assumed enormous significance. It is as if he is saying 'Yes, I know the dots are important, and I am going to make this clear to my readers'.

When peer teaching, Yazan made sure that his pupils remembered to write the dots. On one occasion he was showing his friend Imrul how to write 'Yazan' in Arabic. A dot formed part of one of the letters, but Imrul at first ignored it since to him it was not significant. In the English writing system, a dot is only used on the letter 'i', which can usually be understood without it. Yazan twice reminded Imrul about the dot and pointed out exactly where it should be placed. Finally, Imrul realised that this dot was necessary in Arabic.

Writing accents in Spanish

One way that Spanish differs from English is in its use of accents and other diacritics (marks which affect the sound of a letter or the stress in a word). As in Arabic, these marks are necessary because the word would sound different without them and therefore have a different meaning. An example is the word 'papá' (dad). The accent requires the stress to fall on the last syllable. Without the accent, the word would be 'papa', with the stress on the first syllable, and in Latin American Spanish this means 'potato'.

I recall an incident from another research project in which this difference caused a stir. Spanish-speaking children in London were writing e-mails to penfriends in Chile. Luis, whose family came from Colombia, wanted to ask his Chilean correspondent 'Como se llama tu papá' (What's your father's name?) in Spanish. Unfortunately the e-mail programme did not provide accents. Luis complained when he could only write 'Como se llama tu papa' – 'It says potato!'

Luis' reaction highlights how users of different scripts come to interpret written marks in particular ways. Although I have learned Spanish, I was brought up as a writer of English, so accents hold little significance for me. I found it easy to see 'papa' as 'papá', since they seemed to me very similar. To Luis, however, they were qualitatively different. He was distressed that he appeared to be enquiring the name of his friend's potato, not his father.

Although Sadhana and Brian were not yet being taught about accents at Saturday school, we observed them learning from family members at home. Both children recognised that these features were significant, and were formulating ideas about how they might work.

Brian's eight-year-old brother Julian, who was his close companion and teacher, showed him that an accent on a letter meant stressing that part of the word. When helping Brian to write the word 'mamá' (mum), Julian shouted out the accented syllable to emphasise it, and stated 'es más duro' (it's harder): in other words an accent leads to a stronger sound, which Julian signified by using loudness.

When Brian was working with his mother at home, he once wrote the word 'papá' as 'papa'. The following exchange then took place in

Spanish. His mother reminded him about the accent by asking 'What's missing? ... a little stick here on top, so that it sounds like 'pa*pa*" (emphasising the stress on the second syllable as she said the word). Brian showed his understanding by shouting out the second syllable as he read the word 'nené' (baby).

Children also need to learn about the letter 'ñ' in Spanish (as in the word 'España'), which has a different pronunciation from the letter 'n'. In the same session, Brian's mother helped him to write 'niña' (girl), sounding out the 'ñ' as she did so. She told him 'it's the N but what has it got on top? It's the one that has a little stick like this' (writing the diacritic above the 'n').

Two months later, Brian encountered these issues again when using a set of cardboard alphabet letters to write words. His grandmother was on hand to help. The set included small pieces of cardboard to represent the two types of diacritic: straight lengths for accents and curly-shaped pieces to place over the letter 'n' to make 'ñ'. Brian picked out a curly-shaped piece and placed it above the first 'a' in 'papá'. He had remembered that the word 'papá' needed 'a little stick' of some kind, but was still in the process of sorting out the meanings of the two different 'little sticks' and deciding which of the 'a' letters in the word required this extra sign.

His grandmother guided him to pick the piece of cardboard representing the accent instead, saying in Spanish 'It's an accent (una tilde) that you put on top of the 'a' – it makes the sound hard'. Later, when making the word 'niña', Brian grabbed the correct sign to place above the second 'n' and sounded out the word 'ni ... nya ... nya'. He was beginning to clarify the purpose of each type of diacritic.

'A different N, it's a different N'

Next day, Brian himself was the teacher and his friend Charlie the pupil in a peer teaching session at primary school. The children were using the set of cardboard alphabet letters, and also doing their own writing with pen and paper. When preparing to teach Charlie, Brian formed 'niño' with the cardboard letters, choosing the curly-shaped piece of cardboard and placing it correctly. When writing the word 'muñeco' (doll) himself, he drew the same diacritic above the letter 'n' to look like the piece of cardboard, rather than using a thinner line as would be expected in print.

Figure 31: Brian's writing of the Spanish letter 'ñ' and the word 'mamá'.

Later in the same session, Brian repeated this style of representation (see Figure 31) when I asked him if any letters in the Spanish alphabet were different from English. He told me 'They [i.e. English people] haven't got a N with *this* on top...' and wrote a capital N with the enlarged diacritic above, saying 'There, 'enye''. Charlie found this idea strange and queried: 'What, if you wanna write N you have to put one of them?' and Brian emphasised 'A different N, it's a different N'.

Brian also told Charlie the purpose of the cardboard accent: 'you use it for – to speak loud' (saying these words more loudly, to show what was meant). When I asked him to demonstrate how he would use it in writing, Brian wrote 'mama', then drew an elongated oval – just like the cardboard version – above the second 'a' (see Figure 31) and suddenly shouted 'mamá', stressing the final syllable.

Brian's representation of the diacritic in the letter 'ñ' (a difficult mark to write) is curlier than the accent in 'mamá'. He had taken note of the two shapes and was aiming to show the difference. Why did he make them so large? He had just been handling the cardboard shapes, and seems to have transferred the feeling of tangible bulk onto paper. Written in this way, the diacritics also look more like the 'little sticks' mentioned by his mother than narrow lines would do. And, like Yazan with his enlarged versions of the dots in Arabic, Brian was drawing attention to the importance of these marks in carrying meaning.

Exploring symbol design

Young children notice that handwriting and print are produced in different styles. For example, in Arabic the dots can be represented as either diamond-shaped or spherical in print, whilst in rapid handwriting they become more like short dashes. The size of the dots relative to the other parts of the letters can also vary. Children enjoy experimenting with a range of styles and exploring the limits of variation. They have to work out how far they can go before a symbol changes so significantly that the meaning is altered.

In Figure 32 we see Yazan exploring different possible forms of the letter 'tha' in his Arabic school exercise book. In the example given on the right-hand side of the page, the dots are diamond-shaped and the rest of the letter consists of a curved semi-circle which varies in thickness at different points in the curve, as it would do if written with pen and ink. It therefore already differs in certain ways from the version which a teacher would write in pencil, biro or board pen.

In the lined space on the left-hand side, Yazan was supposed to follow this example. Rather than repeating one version only, Yazan has produced many versions, each slightly different in shape, angle and relative size of the features involved. He is playing with the form: could it look like a boat, or a box? Could the dots be rounded or spiky? The possibilities seem endless, and of course many of these forms would be recognisable if used in stylised print or individual handwriting. They are variations on a theme, rather as a composer would explore the potential of a musical phrase.

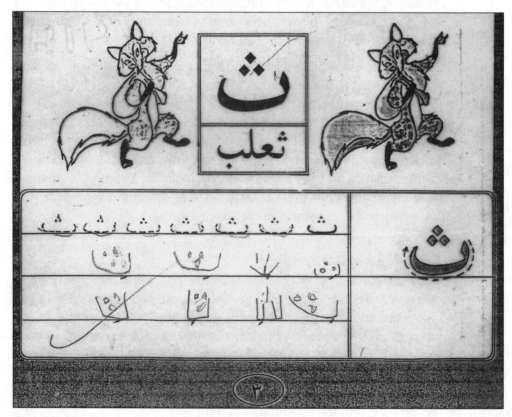

Figure 32: Yazan's many versions of the Arabic letter 'tha'.

Making your mark

Children also like to develop their own style, particularly when writing their name. Producing a signature is the most personal and self-defining act of writing, and children recognise it as such. This can explain why children's signatures are often unconventional. Brian, for example, wrote his name in a combination of upper- and lower-case letters. It could be assumed that this was because he was still working out the difference between the two types of lettering. However, it also seems that this particular representation of his name became important to Brian, because he continued to use it throughout the year of the research project.

Part of his signature involved the upper-case form of the letter 'N'. Brian was especially attached to this form of 'N' when writing other words too, probably because he linked it with his name. Figure 33 shows a worksheet in which Brian was expected first to trace words which came from a story, then cover the example and write it again from memory, then check back with the example and write a final version.

Brian has complied with the first instruction: all his words in the first column follow the model provided. However, as soon as he writes each word for the second time, he uses the capital 'N' – and when required to check back with the model, he persists with that letter throughout. It is unlikely that Brian could not recognise the difference between the lower- and upper-case letters. Rather, his form of the 'N' held personal significance and he preferred to keep to it in his own writing.

Children often feel strongly about their particular design of a written symbol and are prepared to argue for it. At stake is the issue of social acceptability – does their version fall within the boundaries of conventional meaning? – and also the desire to produce an individual flourish. We can see this in a discussion between Brian and his classmate Charlie about how to write the lower-case letter 'a'.

Brian's versions of 'a' tended to have a long 'tail', as shown in the last letter of 'mamá' in Figure 31. Charlie disputed this design when he was asked to write Spanish words based on Brian's examples, saying 'But do the A's right, no let me do the A's actually'. He then asked Brian 'How do you do the A's? ... 'cos you don't do them how *I* do it', recognising that different versions were possible. However, he renewed his challenge as Brian finished writing the next word, grabbing Brian's exercise book and arguing 'No you don't do it like that – I do it even nicer'. Brian wrote

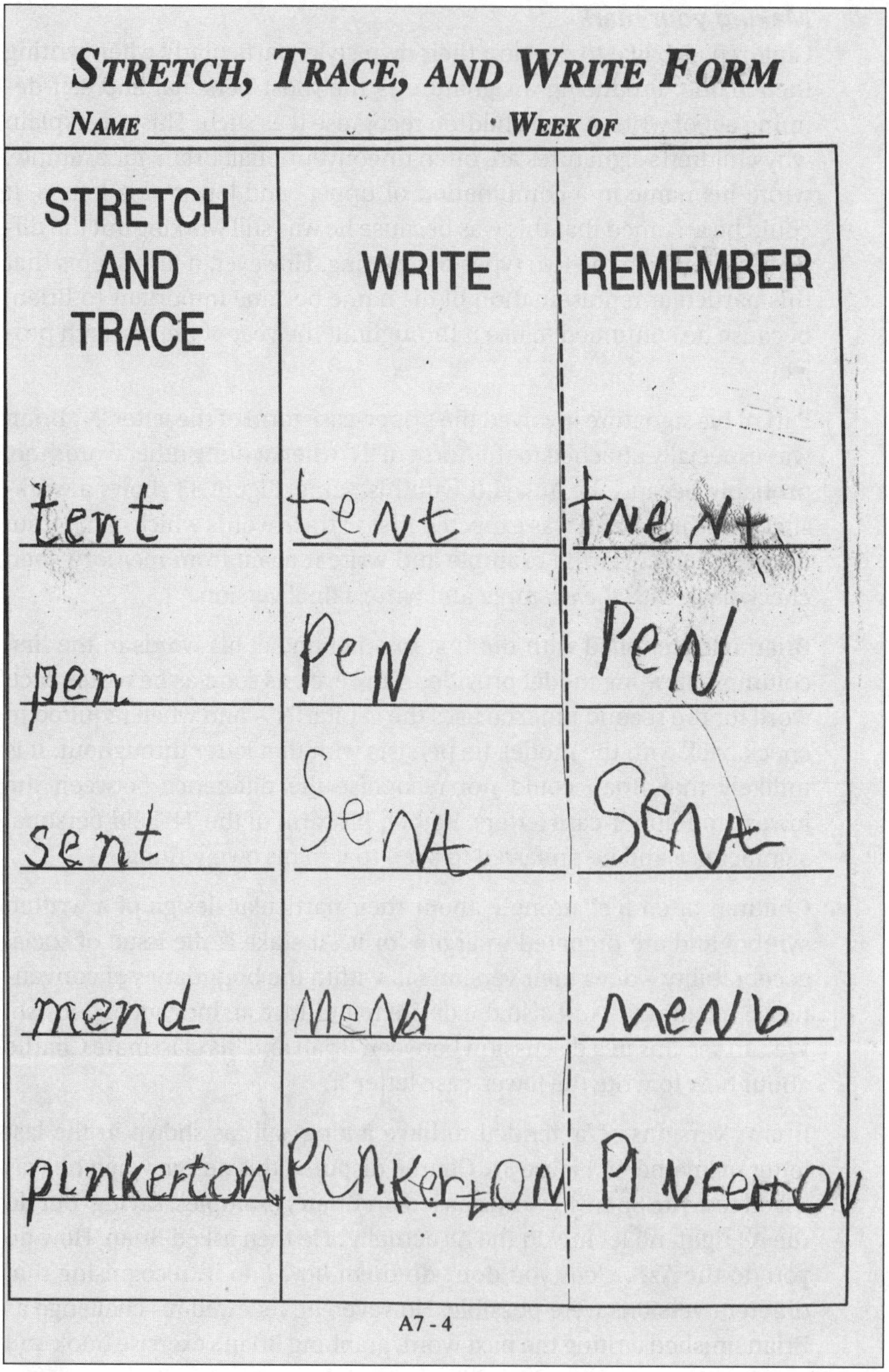

STRETCH, TRACE, AND WRITE FORM

NAME _____ · WEEK OF _____

STRETCH AND TRACE	WRITE	REMEMBER
tent	tent	tnent
pen	PeN	PeN
sent	SeNt	SeNt
mend	MeNd	meNb
pinkerton	PLNKertON	PI NFettoN

A7 - 4

Figure 33: Brian's preference for the upper-case letter 'N'.

another 'a' with a long tail, insisting 'I do my A's like this', and Charlie negotiated a compromise, saying 'I like Brian's A's too, it's just different to *my* way'. The exchange finished with Charlie stating 'That's how I do my A's' as he completed an 'a' with an elegant flourish, though a rather more traditional tail.

The boys' involvement in this discussion shows the personal investment young children make in symbol design. Their explorations are partly shaped by the teaching they have experienced – as he wrote the letter 'a', Brian was heard to say 'go round and down...', remembering the advice of his primary school teacher. At the same time, each child develops an individual interpretation of how symbols can be written. Thus Brian maintained the right to give a 'tail' to his 'a', so that it stood out from convention.

Identifying the issue

As we have seen, children identify certain issues as significant when learning about writing systems, and cogitate about these concepts until they are eventually clarified. Symbol design is no exception. Certain symbols, for example, look very similar and it can take time for children to sort out which is which. However, they are likely to recognise that care needs to be taken to get it right.

When Sadhana was teaching her classmate Nicky about Spanish writing, the two children were first putting a set of cardboard alphabet letters in order. At this point, Sadhana had the English alphabet in mind, singing the song beginning 'ABCDEFG...' as she organised the letters. Nicky asked 'is B second – A, B?' Sadhana answered 'yeah', putting the letter 'd' in second place. The cardboard letters were in lower case; therefore 'd' and 'b' looked similar to her. However, she then looked again and commented 'no, that's a P – oh yeah, that's a B'. From the angle where she was sitting, 'p' was another possibility for the letter she had just put down. Sadhana continued to mull over the issue, saying under her breath 'P, oh, B'.

Shortly afterwards, the children reached 'D' in the alphabet sequence and Nicky was looking for this letter. Sadhana picked up a letter 'b' and held it upside down. She asked me 'is that a D – or a P?' She continued to turn the letter around, looking at me and saying 'what can this be? I think it's a ... D'. Indeed, this particular shape can stand for either 'b', 'd' or 'p', depending on its orientation. In her question 'what can this be?',

Sadhana captured the idea that a shape can have different potential meanings, metamorphosing from one letter into another. She also knew what the possibilities were in this case, even if she was not yet sure which was which.

Nicky then joined the debate by pointing to the letter 'b' and saying 'that's a D, that's a D!' Sadhana agreed. Nicky continued 'a B's that way', gesturing to the left – but then also to the right – 'and a D's are that way' (gesturing to the right). He did not seem certain of the precise orientation of lower-case 'b' and 'd', but knew that one had the loop to the left and the other to the right.

Both children were in the process of working out this distinction, a tricky one for emergent writers. Teachers and family would have been giving advice, but each child needed to come to their own conclusions over a period of time. Meanwhile, their discussion revealed awareness of which letters needed to be distinguished, and the key features involved. They showed considerable interest in this matter, spending around half an hour sorting out the entire alphabet.

Spatial location
Writing Chinese characters: 'make sure it's centred'
Every Chinese character is harmoniously balanced around a central point. So when writing, the space for constructing each character is visualised as an empty square. The first stroke has to be placed quite precisely with respect to the centre of the square, in order to occupy the correct space in relation to strokes that follow. Each subsequent stroke can then be placed in its exact location, until the whole stroke pattern has been built up successfully.

To help children learn to see space in this way, Chinese school exercise books are divided into squared grids and each character is written in one square. Some schools use books where each square in the grid is sub-divided into four or eight sub-sections, so that strokes can be placed even more precisely.

Ming was in the first year class in his Chinese school, and his teacher drew a grid on the board every time she wanted to present a new character. The stroke sequence was built up with each step being shown in one square of the grid, as seen earlier in this chapter in the page from Selina's exercise book (Figure 24). Children first followed this sequence and then practised the whole character in each square. Teachers gave few verbal instructions about the balance of the character; children learned mainly through the visual example. On one occasion Ming's teacher explicitly advised: 'make sure it's centred'. As children were writing a character, they might realise they had begun in the wrong place with respect to the centre of the square, and rub out their work and start again.

Selina's teacher in the second year class no longer used a grid on the board, although the children's exercise books still had squared pages. By this point, children were expected to visualise the imaginary squares in which the teacher was placing her characters, and balance their own writing of strokes in their exercise books accordingly. In addition, the squares in the second year exercise books were smaller than those in the first year books, requiring the children to develop increased pen control and more detailed visual understanding in order to write characters on a smaller scale.

When peer teaching, Selina and Ming both used a whiteboard and demonstrated that they saw the space for writing Chinese as consisting of centred squares. Selina presented characters to her 'pupils' on the board without providing a grid, since she was already able to imagine the squares. She could produce well-balanced characters under these conditions, but her primary school classmates found it difficult to emulate her. They were not used to interpreting space as centred, being only accustomed to the linear arrangement of English writing, but Selina was easily able to switch to a centred spatiality when writing Chinese.

Ming usually drew a grid when teaching his peers, except on one occasion, when he had also written the character much smaller than usual. When I remarked on the size, he explained that it was because of the boxes. When I said 'But you haven't done any boxes', he pointed out that the boxes were already there. I looked closely at the whiteboard and there was indeed a grid of small squares in the material underneath the surface layer, which I would not otherwise have noticed. These squares were visible to Ming because he was looking out for them – to him, this was how the page would be planned in Chinese.

Linearity in Arabic, Spanish and English

Words in English, Arabic and Spanish occupy space in a different way from Chinese characters. Each word consists of a sequence of alphabetic letters joined together in a line. Children are therefore provided with horizontally-lined exercise books or worksheets to encourage them to visualise and use the space on the page in this particular way.

The English, Spanish and Arabic schools in the research project often provided worksheets with banded horizontal lines for handwriting, closely positioned in parallel to each other. The aim was to train children to place their letters between the lines (as in Ming's English class, Figure 34). For each letter, some parts were supposed to be written within the central band, whilst other parts of the letter might reach up into the band above or down into the one below.

Brian's Spanish teacher explained to her pupils that these different lines would help them keep letters in the correct proportion to each other. For example, with the name 'Eduardo', the letters 'u', 'a', 'r' and 'o' should keep within the central band. For 'E' and 'd', the main part of the letter was to be placed in the central band, whilst 'the branch that goes higher' would reach into the top band. For a letter such as 'p' the 'branch' would reach down into the lower band. In Arabic school, workbooks for beginners had one line only, with three bands being provided as the balance of children's handwriting was expected to become more precise.

The children teaching Spanish or Arabic to primary school classmates expected their pupils to write in horizontal lines, although they did not comment if the writing wandered at a slight angle. Occasionally they asked their peers to write words in columns, as when Tala instructed her friends to practise her model word 'mama' with the instruction 'copy it

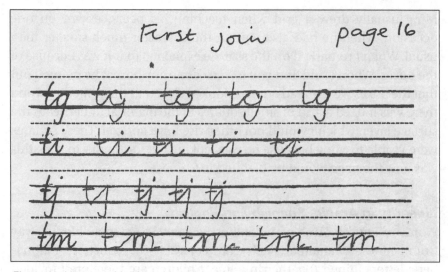

Figure 34: Lines provided to guide handwriting in Ming's primary school class.

all the way down to here', placing a mark at the bottom of the page where they could stop. Such columns were a typical way to practise a single word in Arabic school, and are sometimes used for this purpose in English schools too.

Directionality
Vertical or horizontal?

Because words in English, Spanish and Arabic are written in a line, it is easier to read them horizontally than vertically. It is possible to understand a printed word in English or Spanish if it is written vertically (such as a street sign saying 'restaurant'), but it would be difficult to read a long sequence. Arabic words almost always consist of joined-up letters which have to be read horizontally.

Chinese, however, is a logographic script in which each character represents a separate concept. This means that a Chinese sentence can be written with the characters in horizontal lines or in vertical columns. When learning Chinese, Selina and Ming became familiar with reading and writing both horizontally and vertically. Their exercise books, and some of their textbooks, used the more traditional vertical column arrangement (as seen in Figure 24). Their teachers used vertical columns when presenting stroke sequences for new characters. However, children were also asked to demonstrate stroke sequences in horizontal lines when doing their twice-termly tests, and they wrote and read sentences in the modern horizontal style during lessons.

Selina demonstrated her ability to use both vertical and horizontal Chinese writing. The red paper banners adorning her home for Chinese New Year carried greetings written in traditional vertical columns. Selina read out the message from a similar banner to her friend Ruby in a peer teaching session. Later, she made a New Year card in which she wrote the same message horizontally across the front.

Ming used vertical columns to show his primary school classmates how to build up and practise Chinese characters. As mentioned earlier (see Figure 27), he also produced 'tests' for his pupils like those used in Chinese school, featuring a set of squares running horizontally in which they had to demonstrate each step of the stroke sequence for a given character. Like Selina, he could conceptualise writing and reading horizontally or vertically in Chinese.

Right or left?

English and Spanish are written from left to right, whereas Arabic is written from right to left. Although in theory each script could operate in either direction, visual conventions have grown up which make it difficult to read or write the other way round. Chinese consists of individual characters that can more easily be written in either direction. Traditional Chinese texts with vertical columns (written from top to bottom) move from right to left across the page, whilst modern-style ones with horizontal lines read from left to right. These directionalities can be combined within the same text. In Chinese newspapers, for example, the title of an article might be written either vertically or horizontally, whilst the content might be in right-left columns or left-right lines.

The Chinese school exercise books belonging to Ming and Selina used columns, and therefore operated from right to left. Selina and Ming made sure their pupils in peer teaching sessions opened the exercise books from the right. If their classmates then started in the top left-hand corner of the page, they would correct them by pointing to the opposite corner or telling them 'you have to start here'.

To show the direction in which the characters must be practised, Ming and Selina would move a finger down the columns, going across the page from right to left. Selina was strict with her classmates about this, whereas Ming allowed more latitude. However, he showed that he knew the conventions: for example, when Amina began to fill the squares horizontally he commented 'she's going across!'

Selina and Ming seemed to have no difficulty adapting to the varied directionalities of Chinese script. For certain purposes, such as showing the stroke sequence to build up a character, vertical columns could even be used from left to right; Selina wrote in this way when demonstrating a long stroke sequence on the whiteboard. Similar flexibility was shown by Ming's cousin, Ling, who was in the same class at primary school. Although she attended a different Chinese school where exercise books used the horizontal left-right system, Ling quickly adapted to the vertical right-left system in Ming's exercise books. She noticed when she had forgotten to start on the right after turning to a new page. And when Ming gave her a stroke sequence to write, she checked with him 'You have to do it downways or across?'

Tala and Yazan showed similar flexibility through their experience of writing in both Arabic and English. We have seen that they were aware that Arabic was written from right to left and English from left to right. The children therefore had two potentials for directionality and often used both when doing their own emergent writing. Tala wrote on both covers of her exercise book for Arabic school, because from her dual perspective both had the potential to be the front. Exercise books used by Yazan and his sister Lana at home started at both ends. For example, one began with the Arabic alphabet at the right hand end and the English alphabet at the left hand end.

The children persisted in using both directionalities even though most resources available to them were designed for use from left to right. The Flintstones exercise book seen in Figure 35 had a picture on the 'English' front, while at the other end of the book the manufacturers had left the cover blank. They intended it to be the back cover of a monodirectional English text, but Lana and Yazan decided that the book could be bilingual and bi-directional. Lana wrote Yazan's full name, Yazan Sibay, in Arabic in the blank space, thus claiming it as the Arabic cover. She also wrote his name in English across the picture on the English cover.

We then see Yazan making a fascinating experiment with directionality. Just below his sister's writing of his name in Arabic, he has written it in English, but with Arabic directionality. This is his own creation rather than a reversed copy of Lana's English version – he has used different styles of letter in his first name, and capitals instead of lower case in his second name. Lana has written his name in English again below, perhaps to remind him that English has left-right directionality. However, it seems unlikely that Yazan was confused about this. He often wrote his name in English at primary school, from left to right.

By writing his name in this way, Yazan seems to be exploring the possibilities of directionality, asking himself 'What happens if you write English from right to left?' On another occasion, I saw him writing his sister's name, Lana Sibay, in English script, with 'Lana' written from right to left and 'Sibay' from left to right. This seemed a deliberate way of trying out directional potential.

Many young children, monolingual or bilingual, experiment with reversed directionality in their early writing and like Yazan, are expert at producing this 'mirror writing' – which adults find difficult to do. If children become biliterate in scripts with different directionalities, such visual and actional flexibility is reinforced rather than being channeled into one direction only.

The kinaesthetic process of writing

Handwriting involves physical engagement with script, and this contributes to children's understanding of what each symbol stands for. As well as learning about script visually (through looking at the detail of symbols and the way they are placed on the page), children also learn verbally (through talk about what each symbol represents) and kinaesthetically (through the act of creating symbols). The combination of these modes of learning is powerful.

The kinaesthetic process of writing was taught somewhat differently in the children's Chinese, Arabic, Spanish and English schools. In Chinese class, children learned to build up characters from short separate strokes, each with a precise length and angle. At the Arabic school, the writing process involved a continuous pen action. Each alphabet letter was written as a flowing whole, and the flow continued as letters were joined to make words.

In the Spanish school, each letter was practised in cursive form, in a flowing movement without the pen being lifted from the page. The teacher explained that this was a necessary preparation for joining letters together to form words, and that the ability to write fluidly depended on *motricidad* – a key principle of teaching writing in Spanish. The nearest translation of this word in English would be motor skills, but the meaning seemed much richer, nearer to the French concept of *le graphisme* already discussed.

In the English primary schools, a more mixed process was observed. There was a considerable variety of approaches to the teaching of handwriting. In one school, cursive writing was not taught until children were eight years old, whilst in another, seven year olds were expected to join up their letters in all their written work – although the teacher's own handwriting showed a mixed style, using both print and cursive. Most schools taught the cursive form of letters in specific handwriting sessions, which usually lasted about ten minutes and happened no more than once a day. However, children rarely used cursive writing outside these official sessions, usually printing each letter separately.

In a writing session in Ming's English school (see Figure 34), the teacher emphasised the use of a continuous hand movement: 'for joined-up

opposite: *Figure 35: Lana has written Yazan's name in English on the 'English' cover of the exercise book, and in Arabic on the Arabic cover. Yazan has then experimented by writing his name in English with Arabic directionality ('Flintstones' image adapted and re-drawn by Jenny Travell).*

writing, don't take your pencil off the paper till you finish your letters'. In some schools, children were given exercises involving patterns to practise a flowing hand movement, such as a repeated chain of loops moving along the line. Similar exercises were found in the Spanish school materials, and also in the Arabic school (with slightly different patterns – and different directionality).

Brian's teacher at Spanish school explained to me the philosophy of *motricidad*, which is seen as an integral part of building a bodily disposition towards writing. She described how *motricidad* could be developed through physical exercises, such as drawing large circles in the sand with a stick, although English playgrounds were sadly lacking in the resources suitable for performing these activities compared to her native Colombia. However, she managed to integrate many aspects of *motricidad* into her classroom sessions. For example, she asked children to hold a sheet of paper in the air and tear it into narrow vertical strips, and then tear each of these into tiny pieces which could be picked up individually and made into mosaic alphabet letters. This required considerable visual and bodily co-ordination and dexterity. Another exercise for building strength and flexibility was the recitation of the rhyme *Bate, que bate el chocolate* (stir, stir the chocolate) about stirring a thick hot chocolate drink, accompanied by a circular movement of the wrist.

Lateralidad (directionality) was also considered an important concept to teach in Spanish school, and a good deal of work was done on this through songs and games. Once again this was because of the principles of *motricidad*; a concept needed to be built up through physical activity as well as mental exercises. So games involving instructions such as 'touch your left eye' aimed to help children to clearly identify the left side of their body, and thus to more easily apprehend the difference between letters such as 'b' and 'd'.

Since the body and the mind are linked through the acquisition of *motricidad*, Brian's teacher believed that the action of forming each letter helped children to recognise and remember it. Via the act of writing, children would inscribe the letter in the mind. She stated this explicitly to her pupils when they were working on the letter 'm': 'write the letter in your head'.

Thus the teacher spent considerable time on activities relating to individual letters. For example, when teaching the letter 'o', she asked children to trace it in the air and on the surface of the table, in bigger and smaller circles, and the action was reinforced by drawing pictures of snail shells in a spiralling motion. As the children traced or wrote the 'o', the teacher emphasised that this particular letter needed to start by going to the left, otherwise when children began to write *a mano escrita* (in cursive) they would not be able to join it up to the next letter. Similarly, as children practised the letter 'm', they followed the verbal instructions of 'down, up...' and so on.

Handwriting lessons in English and Arabic school also involved verbal instructions about letter directionality, combined with a visual demonstration. For the joining of 't' to 'o' in Ming's English school, the teacher told the children 'go straight down, it's straight round over the 'o', give your 'o' a little tail, then cross your 't''. The philosophy of connection between physical action and mental processes, however, seemed most developed in the Spanish school.

Linking kinaesthetic and visual

If the act of writing letters is linked with a visual metaphor, this can aid children in their efforts to connect shape and meaning. Teachers at the Arabic, Spanish and English schools described ideas that could help children remember the sounds of different letters and link them to word meaning. The picture alphabet beginning 'A is for apple' is a traditional example, and a similar approach was used in Arabic and Spanish. Sometimes visual attributes of a letter are explicitly compared to the word in question, as when Brian's teacher in English school told her pupils 'the letter S is a lovely easy letter to write – it's just like a snake'. The hissing sound made by a snake – 'sssss' – can also be invoked as another way to reinforce the letter-sound link. The origins of letters may indeed lie in such metaphors, since the alphabet evolved from pictographic writing.

In Spanish school, Brian's teacher described how to write the lower case letter 'd' by telling children first to write 'la bombita' (the little bubble) and then 'el palito' (the little stick). They needed to join these together in the right way: 'if the little bubble is left open, an elegant little stick will fall from it'. The action of the hand in inscribing the letter was closely connected with visual meaning.

Meanwhile, a number of parents and teachers helped children to remember Arabic alphabet letters by grouping them into similar-looking

Figure 36: Three letters which Tala's teacher encouraged her to remember as 'sisters' (they differ only in the number of dots) – and the letter that looked like a duck.

ones, called 'sister' letters. Tala explained this concept to her primary school classmates: 'You see this letter and this letter? They're sisters', pointing to the three letters shown in Figure 36. She then told them that her Arabic teacher said another letter was like 'a duck'. Visual metaphor was also used to help children remember the different forms of letters when they were joined to each other; if the stem of a letter had to be removed or shortened, teachers and parents would say the letter had 'broken a leg'.

Some Chinese characters still retain a direct visual connection with the concepts they stand for, and teachers would refer to these ideas when demonstrating the character on the board. Ming's teacher introduced the character for 'mountain' by writing its three vertical lines, the middle one of which is taller than the others, and then drawing three 'peaks' around the lines. Selina's teacher drew a face with tears running down it, and showed how to convert that into a stylised version which became the character for 'cry'. Other characters, however, were more abstract and were taught through an emphasis on stroke sequence and pattern.

The teachers in children's community language schools and in their primary schools thus combined the visual, verbal and kinaesthetic modes in different ways to help them learn about writing. For each script, the visual and actional processes of producing written symbols were intimately linked with the processes of 'understanding writing' and 'becoming a writer'.

Embodied knowledges

From their experience of different scripts, the children in the research project were developing different kinds of knowledge in several areas: ways of designing symbols and using the graphic space of the page, and the physical process of writing. The term 'embodied knowledges' can be used to describe this learning, because it simultaneously involves visual, actional and cognitive aspects.

Embodied knowledges are part of understanding how a writing system works. As well as knowing what symbols stand for, children recognise that the visual characteristics of symbols and the actions needed to produce them also hold significance. Take, for example, the Flintstones exercise book cover designed by Yazan and his sister (Figure 35). Yazan might have thought 'I can write letters in English or Arabic to represent the sounds of my name; I can design these letters in particular ways, and place them differently in space'. These are all equally important kinds of meaning – all are types of semiotic resource.

How do young biliterates handle their diverse embodied knowledges? The children realised that their primary school classmates might not have the same expertise in these areas, and sought to give advice. For example, when Tala was faced with the challenge of helping Emily to write a word in Arabic, she noticed that Emily was having difficulty producing the fluid curves typical of Arabic script. Emily interpreted a piece of writing by Tala as looking like 'steps', and her own version looked like angular steps in a staircase. Tala commented 'It's not exactly like that – she's done steps', and to help her friend produce more appropriate writing, she provided a join-the-dots version of the word required.

Ming was explicitly aware of the bodily disposition engendered by becoming a writer of Chinese at his Saturday school, where the process of practising many columns of characters at a time – each with a precise stroke pattern – required intense activity of the hand. When teaching his classmate Amina, he made the offer 'If her hand gets tired, I'll do it'. Amina managed to finish an entire page of the character for 'seven', but sat back with a sigh of exhaustion. Part-way through another page of work she started shaking her wrist, and Ming asked 'Is your hand tired?' and proceeded to finish that page on her behalf.

These biliterate children seemed to adapt to different contexts, drawing on their multisemiotic resources in ways they found appropriate. Mainstream educators sometimes think that children will find it hard to switch between ways of writing in different scripts. For example, it is said that children who have learned the precision of writing Chinese will find it difficult to adapt to the relative freedom of the emergent writing they are encouraged to do in English schools. However, children like Selina who have grown up with Chinese and English develop capacities from both writing systems, and can use either to their advantage.

Selina demonstrated this in a peer teaching session by first showing off her knowledge of complex Chinese characters, writing as fast as she could and building up a good number of them on the whiteboard. Her pupils begged her to go slower because they could not keep up. At the end of the session, Selina rubbed off the characters and began to do a swirling pattern all over the board, using expansive gestures very different from the precise, contained actions required for Chinese writing. She was quite capable of visualising and acting in both these ways, and she enjoyed doing both.

Young biliterate children thus have the opportunity to develop a flexible and comprehensive approach to the act of writing. The different capacities built up from learning each script give children an expanded range of possibilities as writers. For example, the precision developed in learning Chinese can be applied to producing detailed observational drawings. Being able to write and read in different directions is likely to be an advantage when dealing with webpages, where space is often planned in a non-linear way. Experimenting with symbol design, spatiality and directionality should enable children to design multimodal texts which maximise the potential of page and screen. Young learners who are developing a variety of 'embodied knowledges' will be well placed to grasp future communicative possibilities.

Ideas for developing children's writing abilities

■ When teaching about the directionality of books, ask children whether they read and write in scripts that use other directionalities. Ask them to show you which way a book goes in Arabic, for example, and which way the lines go on the page. Or find out whether children know that Chinese can be written in vertical columns as well as horizontal lines. Ask children to bring textbooks and exercise books, or magazines and leaflets in various languages so that they can show the class what directionalities are used. Explicit comparison helps biliterate children to clarify these issues for themselves. It also highlights for all learners the specific directionality of English.

■ Ask children who are learning another language to demonstrate their writing abilities to groups of classmates or to the whole class. For example, Ming and Selina both showed their primary school classes how to write particular Chinese characters. Their classmates practised these on a sheet of paper containing a squared grid, like those used at Chinese school. As their work was inspected by Selina or Ming, the children began to realise that precision was important, and started to notice the length and angle of each stroke and how it was positioned. This is an interesting and motivating way for children to extend their kinaesthetic capacities and sharpen their attention to visual detail, and this has a beneficial effect on their writing in English too. Using fluid curves to join letters in a script such as Arabic, or trying out cursive writing in another Roman script such as Spanish, develops children's abilities to accomplish joined-up writing in English.

■ You may already be using activities like those described in the French approach of *le graphisme* or the Spanish approach of *la motricidad,* to develop children's visual and actional capacities. If you would like to extend this work or compare your ideas with those of others, the following publications may be of interest:

- Thomas, F. (1997) *Une question de writing?* London: Teacher Training Agency.

- Ansell, P., Kitchener, G. and Potter, S. (1994) *The Dance of the Pen: Developing a Cursive Handwriting Style for Children.* Cheshire: Cheshire County Council.

- Sassoon, R. (1990) *Handwriting: the way to teach it.* Cheltenham: Stanley Thornes Ltd.

■ For example, Sassoon recommends using letters made from different textures such as clay and sandpaper, and encouraging children to scoop letter shapes out of soft materials such as cake icing and dough, to enhance 'kinaesthetic reinforcement'. Such activities involve body and mind, so that whilst shaping the letter and feeling its substance children are at the same time learning what that letter stands for.

■ Find out from children what marks are used in different writing systems to show accent or stress (as in 'papá' or 'España' in Spanish), or to differentiate one letter from another (as with dots in Arabic). This can help the whole class to think about the varied ways in which graphic symbols can represent sounds. This process of discovery increases language awareness, preparing children to adopt a flexible attitude when they come to learn new languages in the future.

■ Children will enjoy seeing that punctuation in other writing systems may use similar symbols to English, but in different ways. For example, Spanish uses 'upside-down' question marks at the beginning of a sentence. When Chinese is written vertically in columns, each comma or full stop stands out because it takes its own place in the column. Examining these different uses will lead to discussion about the placing and function of punctuation marks in all languages, including English.

■ The most personal way for children to 'make their mark' is by developing their own signature. This can be done using a variety of symbol design and in different scripts. If children have a fondness for an unconventional use of symbols (as Brian did by insisting on including an upper case 'N' in his name), ask them to talk about this with you. If children know how to write their name in another script, or if their name is written in a Roman script but contains an accent or other marking, ask them to show you how it looks different from English. The whole class is likely to enjoy writing their names in another script with the help of bilingual parents or older siblings. The look and feel of a different script opens up the possibility for entering into other cultural worlds.

4
Living in simultaneous worlds

The cover of this book shows Selina's drawings of her mother and sister, with the words 'I love my mum' and 'I love my sister' written below in English. Above the picture of her mother Selina has written 'love' in Chinese, whilst above her sister's head she has placed Chinese characters representing the concept of 'Girl Power'.

Here Selina has chosen to combine her writing systems, linking images of two of the people closest to her with ideas holding special significance. Love for her mother is expressed in both Chinese and English. 'Girl Power' is a slogan coined in English by one of Selina's favourite all-female Western pop groups, but Selina uses a translation available in Chinese and links the idea to her ten-year-old sister Susannah.

Selina's representation shows us the world of a six-year-old whose life is lived simultaneously in Chinese and English – a world in which symbols and concepts from two languages co-exist. For Selina, these bilingual links are an important part of her emotional and intellectual development. Yet the institutions of our society, including primary schools, tend to separate out the languages in children's lives. Often children are required to use only English at school and other languages are restricted to home and community. The justification usually given is that children will experience confusion if allowed to think and write in more than one language, or that their learning of English will be held back. Our research, however, found a very different story.

The bilingual children in our project were well aware of the differences between their languages and literacies, as many examples in the previous chapters have shown. But they were also interested in exploring connections between these systems. When writing, they had two sets of resources present in their minds and could draw on either or both of them to make a text. This is the potential creativity and learning power of living in simultaneous worlds.

Switching between languages and literacies

It used to be thought that a bilingual speaker or writer would show their competence by always keeping their languages separate. However, researchers have recently begun to investigate the purposeful ways in which people switch between languages, particularly in multilingual contexts. A bilingual child growing up in London in the new millennium, for example, needs to negotiate the complexities of a constantly-changing linguistic and cultural environment. Studies have shown that children become highly competent language users in order to communicate with grandparents who speak one language, schoolfriends who speak another, and parents and siblings who usually speak both. In situations where everyone is bilingual or multilingual, people switch between their different languages within the conversation to maximise communication. Children are active participants in this process of code-switching.

Hayat Al-Khatib (2003) looks at her children growing up through primary school to adolescence, using mainly Arabic at home and at community language school, and English with mainstream school peers. However, they also switch between languages with bilingual friends and with their parents and siblings. At times, this facilitates discussion of their school day or a film they have seen. At other times, they switch in order to accomplish certain personal goals – to insist on ownership of a toy, to assert authority over a younger sibling, or to persuade their mother that their homework is finished and they are now free to go out with friends.

Children and young people also switch between languages as an important way of signalling and constructing their identities. The purpose may be to explore the complexity of their own multilingual and multicultural background, as Roxy Harris (2003) found with London fourteen-year-olds of South Asian origin. Or it may be to forge relationships with peers from other language backgrounds, as Ben Rampton (1995) shows in his study of how adolescents in a London school use 'crossing' between languages to establish interethnic connections.

For similar reasons, children may use more than one language and script in their writing. In my research in a South London nursery class

(Kenner, 2000), I found that four-year-old Meera used both Gujarati and English script in most of her texts. When making pages for a 'travel brochure' for the nursery's roleplay area, she represented India and the northwestern area of Gujarat (where her grandparents lived) in her own versions of English and Gujarati lettering. Meera knew that English was the main language of the primary school, but staff also encouraged her to write in Gujarati and she had Gujarati texts written by her mother alongside her in the classroom. Whilst making the travel brochure pages, she said 'I want to write my Gujarati'. The script was closely connected with the idea of India and with her family life.

When young writers have access to more than one literacy, they may switch within sentences or even within individual words. Aura Mor-Sommerfeld (2002) found examples of children doing this when writing stories and messages in both Hebrew and English. Mor-Sommerfeld could identify their reasons for choosing each script, such as the moments when six-year-old Shiran discovered creative ways of using the English letters 'G' and 'T' to represent sounds in Hebrew. The different directionalities of English and Hebrew presented no problem. Children used techniques such as transferring to the other script on a new line and beginning just below the end of the previous line, so that the writing snaked to and fro across the page (a method which was in fact employed in scripts thousands of years ago).

Mor-Sommerfeld gives this process of combining scripts the apt name of 'language mosaic', and it resonates with the findings of Abdul-Hayee Murshad (2002) about bilingual children's inventiveness with spoken language. Listening to children of Bangladeshi origin in a London primary school playground, Murshad noticed that as well as switching between Bengali and English they were fashioning a new kind of grammar in their talk, drawing on structures from both languages. They would not have used this grammar with a monolingual English speaker – it was a new way of communicating with peers who shared their language background.

Two worlds, multiple worlds, or simultaneous worlds?

It is often said that bilingual children live in two worlds, and have to constantly transfer from one to the other. In this view, each 'world' is seen as relatively stable and predictable, with its own language and culture which differ markedly from those in the 'other world'. However, theorists such as Stuart Hall have pointed out that language and culture are in fact continually changing, and particularly so in current contexts which are often globalised and multilingual.

In these circumstances, we could understand children as living in 'multiple worlds'. Hall suggests that new identities arise as part of this process of change; the 'self' is now 'composed of multiple 'selves' or identities in relation to the different social worlds we inhabit' (Hall, in Morley and Chen, 1997: 226). Hall describes this 'self' as 'fragmented and incomplete' (*ibid*), but is this how bilingual children experience their existence?

Interviews with young bilinguals suggest that they are capable of handling their multiple identities and seeing their varied experiences as beneficial. Jean Mills (2001) conducted a study with third-generation British children of Pakistani origin, and found they could define themselves as having different but co-existing identities. Children and young people in these situations often seek some kind of synthesis, a 'hyphenated identity', as Paul Ghuman discovered in his research (1994) with second-generation teenagers who wanted to be accepted as both British and South Asian.

But have some children's lives moved on from multiple worlds to 'simultaneous worlds'? Children who are growing up with more than one language from birth or from an early age, and who begin learning more than one literacy at the same time, may spend a good deal of their time in settings which are multilingual and multicultural. For these children, it becomes difficult to define which is their first or second language. The language of their parents or grandparents could still be termed their mother tongue, since it is likely to be used by adults for expressing emotional closeness and dealing with the everyday tasks which make up parenting. However, the children themselves may be equally or more fluent in English, which is also likely to be used among the family at home. Their cultural experiences within their homes and communities may be just as varied in relation to music, TV programmes, food and fashion which combine aspects from both cultural origins into a new synthesis.

This would seem a complex existence to people brought up in more monolingual or monocultural circumstances, but the children we observed in our research project seemed to thrive on simultaneity – and indeed, to seek it out and further it through their use of their different writing systems. How did they do so?

Boundaries and crossings

Sadhana, Brian, Yazan, Tala, Ming and Selina were all aware of the boundaries between their two writing systems, recognising key characteristics that differentiated each system from the other. This is shown by instances already discussed, such as Ming commenting on the ways his name was written in Chinese and in English, Selina pointing out the meaning of different parts of a Chinese character, Yazan showing his primary school classmates the directionalities of Arabic and English texts, Tala explaining how Arabic letters change shape when they are joined into words, Sadhana emphasising the importance of vowels in her learning of Spanish, and Brian demonstrating how to link consonants with vowels in Spanish to create syllables.

In peer teaching sessions, the bilingual children often highlighted these differences between English and Chinese, Arabic or Spanish. However, their classmates tended to interpret the new script offered to them by comparing it to symbols from English. For example, when Selina demonstrated Chinese writing to her class, children spotted elements within the characters which they thought they recognised, and made comments such as: 'That's a G!' or 'That's an E!' They seemed hopeful that this might actually be the same symbol as in English.

The biliterate children knew that symbols in Chinese or Arabic were in fact different, holding different meanings. Even in Spanish, letters could have different sounds. By making statements about these issues, the children maintained the boundaries between their two writing systems. Yet in their negotiations with their classmates, they also recognised that some symbols could cross over between systems (though possibly taking on a different meaning).

For example, when Yazan wrote his name in Arabic in a peer teaching session, his friend Imrul commented 'You writed a three, didn't you?' One element of Yazan's name did indeed look like the English numeral '3'. Yazan answered clearly 'No'. But then Imrul suggested that another part of Yazan's name could be a letter 'U'. This time Yazan replied 'No – yeah!' His initial response of 'No' showed that he knew his name was written in Arabic and did not contain an English 'U'. However, by switching to 'Yeah!' he allowed for the fact that part of the Arabic writing bore a resemblance to this English letter.

Later in the same session, Yazan was writing another Arabic word using his Saturday school work as a model (Figure 37). As he wrote, he com-

Figure 37: Yazan and Rahul writing on alternate lines. Rahul followed Yazan's model and received two stars. When writing the word on the third line, Yazan commented on different parts as looking like 'a zero', 'a U' and 'a one'.

mented on various parts of the word, saying 'this look like a zero and this look like a U and this look like a one'. All these comparisons were possible. By using the phrase 'look like' instead of 'is', Yazan showed he knew the symbols were similar in appearance but did not have the same meaning. They co-existed simultaneously in different writing systems.

Ming was careful to ensure that his primary school classmates did not step over the boundaries between Chinese and English. When he was teaching Amina to write the Chinese symbol for 'seven', her writing sometimes began to look too much like the English numeral 'four' (see Figure 38). Ming was concerned that Amina might be seeing the Chinese symbol from an English perspective, so he corrected her: 'That's a four! That's wrong'. In another place, Amina's writing began to cross over into the English lower-case letter 't', and again Ming stated 'That's wrong! That's a T'.

Some symbols, however, do cross boundaries between systems and retain their meanings. One example is a 'tick' symbol, which Ming's teacher used to mark his Chinese work in Saturday school, just as it was used in his English school. A similar-looking symbol also appears else-where in Chinese writing – as one of the stroke types used to build up Chinese characters. Ming's friend Roberto spotted this when looking at the first page written by Ming in his Chinese exercise book, and identi-fied it as a tick. Ming accepted Roberto's suggestion, recognising that this symbol could be used in both systems.

In the children's discussions of what symbols could stand for, they took ideas from letter systems, number systems and other types of graphic symbol such as the 'tick'. On one occasion, Yazan also ventured into the realm of mathematical symbols. He began from Arabic writing, showing a classmate how to write the dots that differentiate certain similar-

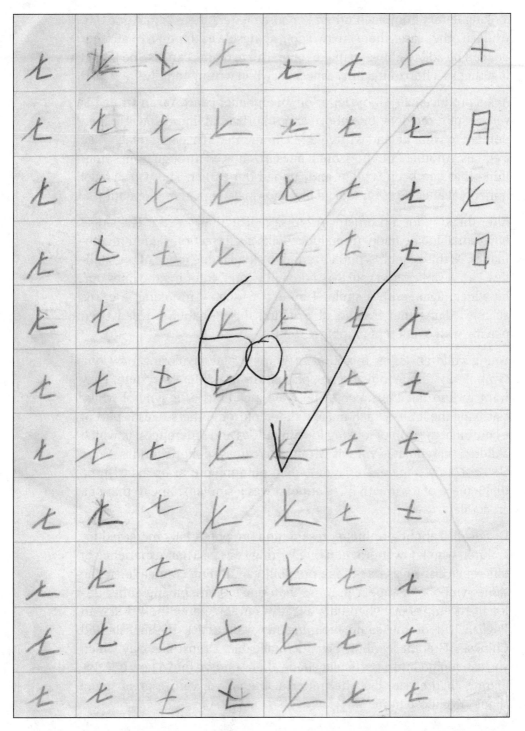

Figure 38: Amina's writing of the Chinese character for 'seven', which Ming commented on when it looked too much like the English numeral 'four' or the English letter 't'.

looking letters from each other. For some letters there is just one dot, while in other cases there are two dots alongside each other, or another dot can be added above to make three. The two dots can also be joined together as a horizontal line, especially when writing rapidly.

As he produced an Arabic letter on an alphabet chart, Yazan wrote his version of three dots: one above and a horizontal line below. He then pointed to what he had written and commented 'This is a equals – like a equals'. Another faint horizontal line also showed through from something that had been written and rubbed out earlier. The two parallel horizontal lines together looked like an 'equals' sign in mathematics.

After thinking for a moment, Yazan said 'like a take-away'. The single horizontal line he had written looked like a subtraction sign in mathematics. At this point his 'pupil' started to laugh at the range of possibilities. Yazan smiled and said 'No, I done it wrong'. Rubbing the lines out, he added, again with a smile: 'I done it wrong – I'm joking!' He was acknowledging that instead of teaching the alphabet, he had been playing with a different graphic system.

Young children enjoy this kind of graphic play, exploring how one symbol can mutate into another, perhaps from a different system. They want to find out the range of possible meanings of a symbol whilst clarifying the limits which make it different from others. This is part of a continual mission of looking for similarities and differences, in which children manipulate symbols within and across semiotic modes; Kress (1997: 87) gives the example of a child pointing out at breakfast-time that a piece of toast with bites out of it was a similar shape to that of a crocodile.

Discoveries about graphic representation are potentially increased for children who know more than one writing system. Their experience of difference also gives rise to the possibility of finding connections. The same symbol can appear in more than one system, having either different meanings (as when part of Yazan's Arabic name looked like an English 'U') or the same meaning (as with a tick in English and Chinese). Graphic symbols become malleable, almost like clay which you can mould into a particular shape, then squeeze into a new one. Biliterate children are like the potter at the wheel, with a great many shapes to choose from.

Drawing on both sets of resources

Since the children in our project had more than one writing system available to them, they had an expanded range of resources to choose from when making a text. They sometimes made use of elements from both systems as they wrote, transferring from one to the other between words or phrases or even within a word. In each case, the child did so in particular ways, for particular reasons.

One example shows how Sadhana could think of the Spanish and English writing systems simultaneously, to the extent that she was able to use them both within a single word. This happened when she was at home with her mother, using cardboard alphabet letters to form English and Spanish words alongside each other. Sadhana was making the word 'girl' in English, which would then be followed by its equivalent in Spanish, 'niña'. She put out the letters g-e-r (she was representing the way girl is pronounced in London English, which sounds more like gel or gerl).

When her mother asked 'What else?', because the word was unfinished, Sadhana said 'niña, we're missing A' and added an 'a' to the letters she had already set out, making 'gera'. She then immediately said 'No, girl! I'm doing a girl, girl!' and started looking for the letter 'l' instead, which would complete the English word.

Whilst producing 'girl', Sadhana was thinking at the same time of 'niña', which also has four letters – and her experience was so simultaneous that the final letter 'a' of 'niña' appeared instead of the English letter 'l'. Also, in Spanish it is important to remember the letter 'a' at the end of certain words because it is used to show the female gender: 'niña' is a girl whereas 'niño' is a boy. This may have influenced Sadhana's decision too.

In her task of placing English and Spanish words next to each other, Sadhana's aim was to investigate how the same concept was represented in each of her writing systems. She knew the meaning was equivalent, but the writing was different. This task heightened her experience of simultaneity as she actively maintained the equivalent word sets in her mind, and led to 'niña' temporarily overlapping with 'girl'. However, Sadhana instantly realised that she was currently writing an English word rather than a Spanish one, and so made the decision to return to 'girl'.

Figure 39: Brian's drawing of a bear with wings, with the caption 'un oso que vuele' (a bear which flies).

A text produced by Brian drew on English and Spanish within the same phrase and even within the same word, but his purpose was different from Sadhana's. Brian wanted to write a complete caption for his picture of a bear with wings (Figure 39). He decided that it should say 'un oso que vuele' (a bear which flies). The first two words did not present many problems. Brian used the number '1' to represent the concept of 'un' – in Spanish 'uno' means '1', and 'un oso' means both 'a bear' and 'one bear', so he could draw on the system of mathematical representation here. The next word, 'oso' (bear) was a complete word already familiar to him.

However, Brian had not yet been taught the more complicated spelling of the words 'que' and 'vuele'. Faced with this challenge, he rose to the occasion by creatively combining his English and Spanish writing systems to make meaning. The English letter name 'K' sounds very similar to the Spanish word 'que', so Brian made use of that next. Similarly, the sound of the English letter 'w', when combined with the Spanish ending 'le', makes a good representation of the word 'vuele'. Neither 'k' nor 'w' usually appears in Spanish, except when representing words from other languages, but Brian employed both letters effectively here. By writing '1osokwle', he achieved his aim of producing a complete text in which all sound-symbol correspondences were accounted for.

Another reason for using more than one writing system in a text is to explore the different potentials of each system, as we saw in the previous chapter when Yazan wrote his sister's name, Lana Sibay, in English but with the first word from right to left and the second from left to right. He was experimenting to see what happened if English script was written with Arabic directionality.

In other cases, the children's use of English directionality when writing Arabic, or vice versa, had a different cause. Because both directionalities were co-present in the children's minds, they sometimes experienced 'moments of transition' when transferring from one system to the other. For example, on one occasion when Tala had just demonstrated the spelling of her name in Arabic, she began her name in English from right to left. She then immediately crossed this out and wrote 'Tala' in English from left to right.

We saw that Tala knew which directions were appropriate for English and Arabic. She often pointed out the difference and corrected her friends in peer teaching sessions. When she began writing her name from right to left in English on this occasion, it was not because of confusion between her two systems but because she was at a transition point between them. Her action of crossing out shows that she recognised this transition point.

Moments of transition can occur for more experienced writers too. Yazan's ten-year-old sister Lana was accustomed to writing in both Arabic and English. When teaching Yazan at home, she began with a spelling test in English and followed it with a test in Arabic. She initially started the Arabic test on the left-hand side of the board, then realised what she had done a few moments later. Like Tala, Lana quickly self-corrected. Children brought up with more than one writing system are accustomed to dealing with both simultaneously and moving fluidly between them.

Representing simultaneous worlds

Children may construct a bilingual text in order to express their sense of living in multiple social and cultural worlds. The text is a way of demonstrating and confirming their experience of simultaneity. In the cases to be discussed here, the children's words and actions make this agenda explicit.

Tala showed a strong desire to link her two writing systems by making the English and Arabic alphabets map onto each other. This was a project she devised and pursued at home on several occasions. She wrote the English alphabet sequence, and then started writing letters from the Arabic alphabet sequence directly above each English letter. Or she began with the Arabic alphabet and tried to map the English letter sequence 'A, B...' onto it.

Tala's sense of connection was well-founded. Just as peoples of the world are inter-connected in history, so are writing systems. The Arabic and English alphabets have a shared source thousands of years ago. Both alphabets start with letters which stand for very similar sounds ('A' and 'B' in English, 'alif' and 'ba' in Arabic). But after that the sounds only match up occasionally.

Tala realised this, but was not to be deterred. She found another opportunity to pursue her goal in a peer teaching session. One of Tala's classmates tried to interpret the unfamiliar Arabic alphabet by using the English system, saying 'A, B, C, D...' and so on as she pointed to letters on an Arabic alphabet chart, whilst moving her finger across each line from left to right. Tala joined in, because although she was aware that two different systems were involved, she wanted to continue with her aim of finding specific links between the alphabets.

The two girls were looking particularly for the letter 'T', because it was the first letter of both their names. Tala showed where you would expect to find the letter 'T' if you recited the English alphabet and followed the Arabic alphabet on the grid from left to right. Then she tried out reciting the English alphabet and following the Arabic grid the other way, from right to left. Neither of these methods gave the answer of the Arabic letter that sounds like 't' (Tala had shown earlier that she knew where this letter was).

Finally, Tala found a way of making an Arabic letter into a T, visually. She explained 'Some of Arabic and English look similar to each other, of the letters' and showed how one particular Arabic symbol 'looks similar to T only if you chop that off' (indicated the detail which would need to be removed) 'and put a line here' (indicating what would need to be added). The result would indeed have looked like an English 'T'.

Tala was clearly aware of what each Arabic and English letter looked like, and the sound they each stood for. Her description of how to transform an Arabic letter into a 'T' was careful and detailed, but she knew it was only possible through a special manoeuvre: it worked 'only if you chop that off'. However, she recognised that the two alphabets were systems with equivalent functions, and as a child using both systems in her everyday life, she was determined to foster any possible links – to emphasise synthesis rather than difference.

Selina was also engaged in finding connections between her writing systems and between the different facets of her cultural life. According to her mother, Selina was always looking out for examples of Chinese writing being used in mainstream English society. She was excited to discover bracelets with Chinese motifs on sale in her local department store when these were fashionable. She also noticed that a member of the Spice Girls pop group had a Chinese tattoo on her arm. Selina's mother explained that these characters stood for the group's slogan of 'Girl Power'.

Greatly interested, Selina asked her mother how to write the characters. The representation of 'Girl Power', a concept from Western popular culture, in Chinese gave rise to something completely new – a synthesis of expression which appealed to Selina because it resonated with her own life experience. Later, she used this writing as the basis for combining Chinese and English messages about Love and Girl Power with drawings of her mother and sister (Figure 40), as discussed earlier in the chapter. By placing the symbols for Girl Power directly above her sister's head, Selina emphasised her view of Susannah – her main role model – as a strong female participant in a Chinese/English world.

At the time Selina produced these drawings, she also made other texts about Love and Girl Power. Figure 41 shows how she repeated the Chinese characters several times on the same page around a central

Figure 41: Selina's drawing of her mother with 'love' in Chinese above, and her sister with 'Girl Power'.

Figure 41: Selina's text about 'Love' and 'Powergirl' alongside the message in English 'I like people kind to me and if they be my friend'.

icon of a heart with the English word 'Love' written above it, and included the word 'Powergirl'. On the opposite part of the page, she drew the heart again, this time framed by butterflies. Pictures of hearts and butterflies often appeared in Selina's texts. This time they were combined with the statement in English 'I like people kind to me and if they be my firend'.

Here Selina has linked Chinese and English writing about love and power with the icons of hearts and butterflies, symbolising love, gentleness and beauty. She represents her bilingual and bicultural life as a happy and well-rounded experience. In this context, Selina's statement about liking 'people kind to me' can be read as a desire for acceptance as a child growing up as both Chinese and English.

Simultaneity at home – and at school?

The examples in this chapter show that if children are in settings where bilingual communication is encouraged, they are able to make creative use of more than one language and literacy. All the children in our project were able to act in this way at home. Their parents wanted them to grow up able to speak and write in their mother tongue but at the same time accepted that English was an important part of their lives.

In a society where English is dominant, children need as many opportunities as possible to use their mother tongue if they are to develop bilingually. Parents recognised this by sending their children to community language school and by using mother tongue as the main means of communication at home. However, English is inevitably used at home and in the community too. The children switched between the two spoken languages with siblings and parents, and literacy activities at home took place in both writing systems.

I described in Chapter 1 the range of cultural experiences taking place in each child's home. Simultaneity in everyday life was expressed and constructed in many different ways: through TV and other media, home decoration and the type of food served at home. Children switched between the news in Arabic and the English children's programme Blue Peter, or between a favourite soap opera from Hong Kong and the English version of Who Wants to be a Millionaire? In Selina's home, decoration on the living room walls included Chinese New Year banners alongside posters of an English pop group. At the evening meal for Ming's family, chicken nuggets and chips were placed on the table alongside Chinese dishes.

Tala's parents explained their views on bringing up children bilingually and biculturally. Her father emphasised the need to be flexible, because children spend most of their day in an English-speaking school environment. Tala's mother estimated that the family spoke Arabic about eighty per cent of the time at home, and the children also spoke English together. With regard to their preferences for food, Tala's father thought the children were 'pure Arab'. He highlighted cultural variety in body language, noting that the actions of Tala and her siblings were more English than Arabic, with less use of hand gestures. However, the children engaged in 'Arabic sitting' (on cushions on the floor rather than on chairs or the sofa) when watching English or Arabic TV programmes. The parents observed their children's range of language use and behaviour with interest, maintaining many aspects of their home culture whilst adapting to a new life in Britain.

Tala and her siblings were at ease with their British Arab identities, as I saw when I visited them at the time of the World Cup football tournament. Tala and her brother Khalid told me excitedly that they had something to show me. They were not quite sure if they should have done it, but they thought 'it's all right because it's in our area'. Wondering what this could be, I followed them outside to the edge of the small car park close to their house. There they had chalked in coloured letters the message 'Come on England'. The children had correctly divined that the minor transgression of chalking on the pavement would be acceptable because their message was part of a wider communal feeling, and because it was in 'our area' – the part of the housing estate which they shared with other neighbours and over which they felt a sense of ownership. For these children, there was no contradiction between the different aspects of their cultural lives, from supporting the English football team to studying the Qur'an or participating in Arabic community celebrations.

When the annual Arabic Community Festival took place at Tala's Saturday school, the British flag appeared alongside those of Arab nations. As the headteacher explained, the school was educating young British Arabs to participate as citizens of a multicultural society. At the Chinese and Latin American Saturday schools, cultural and linguistic mixing also took place. Although the aim was to use the home language as often as possible, children often switched to and fro into English, and teachers used bilingual discussion as a way of clarifying understanding.

The children's mainstream school world was rather different. Although some schools displayed posters in different languages and offered space for the teaching of community languages, the everyday environment was English-dominated. Teachers expressed support for the development of bilingualism and biliteracy, but the curriculum and resources were largely devoted to learning in English. The over-arching framework of the primary school as a monolingual institution tended to restrict children's possibilities for multilingual expression.

The peer teaching sessions showed that the children could demonstrate and develop their bilingual abilities at primary school. Teachers showed their interest in children using both languages and writing systems, and children's 'expert' status was valued and recognised. The artificial separation of having a different code for home and school was temporarily broken down. Children were able to integrate and synthesise their literacy resources, as they would often do at home or in the community.

Different ways of looking at the world

Children growing up bilingual have a range of alternatives available to them in spoken language and in writing. Similarly, their bicultural resources allow them to understand how different groups of people experience and construct the world. Difference is not necessarily a source of difficulty – it is also a stimulus for new ideas. When Yazan and Imrul discussed whether Yazan's Arabic writing contained the English letter 'U', Yazan's response of 'No – yeah!' showed that he was thinking about the possibilities in both writing systems. And when he changed the dots above an Arabic alphabet letter into the symbols for equals and take-away, he was playing with the concepts of difference and connection.

At present, children are given few opportunities at school to play with language and literacy in this way. Society constructs itself as mono-lingual and Anglocentric, and tries to keep children's linguistic and cultural worlds apart. But is this a wise separation? We need to make the most of children's abilities to produce alternative ideas and see a situation from different points of view. If we wish to promote active citizenship, we should value and encourage the experience of living in simultaneous worlds.

Ideas for exploring difference and connection

■ Discuss with children examples of texts written in more than one language: for example, newspapers used in bilingual communities. These are obtainable from local shops, or ask children and parents to bring newspapers, magazines and film posters to school. Ask the class to look at which items are written in English and which in the other language: words in an advertisement, phrases in an article, or whole articles. Why are both languages used? What do those particular words, phrases or articles mean to the community? This exercise can be part of a curriculum activity looking at language as communication, and examining how texts are designed to appeal to their readers.

■ The above activity can also lead on to a discussion about citizenship in which children talk about their bilingual and bicultural lives. Encourage families to bring in photos and videos of celebrations at Saturday school and other community events, and talk about what is happening and what it means to them. What is different about children's experiences in their communities and at primary school, and what is similar? You are likely to find many instances showing the links which already exist, and the discussion will suggest further links that could be made.

■ For children who already know another language or literacy, ask them to use both for classroom tasks or homework. Even if you, as teacher, cannot read their work, children can explain the meanings involved. Do they express themselves in different ways in different languages? Children may need help from parents or other family members to do bilingual work, which enables the family to become involved in homework tasks. It also helps children to think through ideas if they can draw on concepts in both languages.

■ Encouraging children to work in their first language is recommended in National Literacy Strategy training materials on *Supporting Pupils Learning English as an Additional Language* (DfES, 2002) which contain a module on 'Use of first languages in the Literacy Hour', supported by a comprehensive explanation of principles and practice (Bourne, 2002). Other multilingual activities which have been successfully used in classrooms include exploring a West African story in the Literacy Hour to look at text construction in different languages (Gravelle, 2000), drawing on the imagery and metaphor in Bollywood film songs to create poetry (Datta, 2000), using word processing to manipulate different scripts (Edwards, 1998), dual-language book-making (Sneddon, 1993), and connecting with children's home language knowledge to enrich vocabulary learning (McWilliam, 1998).

■ When you see bilingual children writing, you may notice them switching from one system to another, or combining aspects of both systems. For example, children may use a non-conventional directionality for a task. This does not necessarily mean that they are unaware of different directionalities. They may be experimenting, or they may be at a moment of transition between their two systems. Ask children to talk with you about what they are doing, so that you can understand more about how they experience simultaneity in their literacy worlds.

5

Literacy teaching systems in bilingual families

One of Yazan's first teachers was his ten-year-old sister Lana. She often conducted lessons with him, using a small whiteboard propped up against a chair in her bedroom. Yazan would sit on the floor with pen and paper whilst Lana wrote words on the board in Arabic and English, checking his knowledge and helping him with any difficulties. One lesson I observed began with a spelling test in both languages and then Lana and Yazan made a greetings card together. Lana brought out a selection of paper, pens and decorative stickers from a drawer and asked Yazan what kind of card he would like to make. She guided him through the activity and then announced 'I think you're ready to do PE!'

PE involved throwing and catching a ball in the small hallway of the flat. But as Yazan was keen to decorate his card first, he replied 'I'm not ready, Miss'. This response showed his commitment to finishing the task and his acknowledgement of his sister's role as teacher. Lana's persona as the teacher was also emphasised on the day we found a message from her on the whiteboard stating 'Mrs. Sibay is not here today'. Sibay was the children's surname, and the message was written in a manner familiar in their primary school classrooms.

Yazan's mother helped Yazan with reading and writing in Arabic and English, but she told us that Lana was his main teacher: 'she's like his second mother'. Lana acted protectively towards him and she was the family member who knew most about what happened in the English primary school classroom. She also decided to support his learning of

Arabic, going into his Saturday school class each week to check with the teacher how she could best help Yazan at home.

The tasks for bilingual families when their children are learning to read and write are complex, as many want their children to become literate in a community language as well as English. To achieve this dual goal, the skills of family members – parents, siblings and grandparents – are harnessed in whatever combination works best. The skills available in different families may complement each other in different ways. Each family therefore operates as a literacy eco-system, working together in a particular pattern to foster children's learning. Like biological eco-systems, these patterns are dynamic and open to change as families adapt to their current environment. This chapter considers the variety of ways in which literacy eco-systems can operate.

Working together as a family unit

In families around the world, family members work together as a group to accomplish the necessary goals of daily life. Children are inducted into the part they are expected to play. Usually, the adults are the teachers and the children the learners. Barbara Rogoff (1990) describes how young children learn from other family members in various societies: by taking part in practical tasks such as preparing food, by gaining craft expertise such as weaving, and by participating in literacy activities such as book-reading. The skills children learn are appropriate to the aims the family is currently trying to fulfill. In a new setting, family aims and roles may change, but what continues is the need to work together.

When a family arrives in a new country, they have to work out how to manage in another language and literacy, in this case English. If the adults are not yet fluent in the new language, they often turn to earlier arrivals who are more settled and can offer support. Mike Baynham (1995) has described how these other community members act as 'mediators' of language and literacy. David Barton and Sarah Padmore (1994) showed that people with literacy needs rely on a 'network' of such mediators – including relatives and friends – to help them.

As the children grow up in the new country, they become familiar with English through attendance at school, and also find out how language and literacy are taught in the educational system. Soon they start to act as mediators of English for the adults in the family, thus becoming an important part of their family's literacy network. Researchers have found that it is often older siblings, rather than parents, who take on the role of teaching English to younger children at home, just as Lana taught Yazan.

Eve Gregory, Ann Williams and Ali Asghar asked children aged nine to eleven to tape record activities they enjoyed doing with younger siblings. A number of the children were from Bengali-speaking families in London's East End. The activity most chose to record was 'playing school' in English, with the older sibling as teacher. Each activity was impressive in its length and scope, as the older child led a lesson on topics ranging from poetry writing to homophones (Gregory, 2001).

Whilst children often take the lead in helping younger siblings with English, adults have a greater facility in the family's first language and tend to be the main resource for teaching it. Adults also have greater life experience and knowledge in many areas which children have yet to acquire. Parents, grandparents, and aunts and uncles may all be called upon to support certain aspects of learning, depending on their expertise. Dinah Volk describes, for example, how the parents and older siblings of a Puerto Rican five-year-old growing up in the midwestern United States worked together so that 'their joint activities formed a co-ordinated system of caretaking and teaching' (Volk, 1999:29). Such activity, together with the input of others in the extended family and the community, forms a 'mediating network' for literacy learning which benefits young children (Volk and de Acosta, 2004).

Further changes come about in the organisation of a bilingual family's teaching and learning network as their children grow up and become the next generation of parents. By this point, they are confident speakers and writers of English, whilst the grandparent generation often becomes the key resource for supporting children's development in the community language. Families who wish to maintain both languages have to adopt new strategies for doing so.

Families as literacy eco-systems

The families who participated in our research project were first generation arrivals in Britain. They all faced the challenge of adapting to an English-dominant society while also trying to ensure that their children became literate in Chinese, Arabic or Spanish. This was not easy, because the teaching of languages other than English to young children was left entirely to voluntary-run community language schools. The environment for children's bilingual learning was somewhat hostile. As Tove Skutnabb-Kangas (2000) has argued, linguistic diversity is threatened in such contexts, just as biological diversity is threatened in an environment that becomes hostile to certain species.

So it was particularly important that the family worked together to support literacy learning in both languages. David Barton, in his analysis of 'the ecology of written language', suggests that 'the family is an ecological niche in which literacy survives, is sustained and flourishes' (1994: 149). He points out that literacy learning is a dynamic process which can change as new relationships arise between individuals, groups and their social environment.

We could see this happening with the families in our research project. Each family went about the task of supporting their children's bilingual literacy learning in a different way. The specific knowledge of different family members affected their approach, as did factors such as siblings' age and gender, or family size. In some cases, approaches changed over time as a new balance of knowledge and relationships emerged within the family.

The families could therefore be seen to operate as literacy eco-systems. In biology, eco-system is the term given to a group of species that is mutually dependent. For the system to work well, its components need to inter-relate in a balanced way. The eco-system is also dynamic and adjusts to new circumstances. The metaphor of literacy eco-system helps us to understand how family members are mutually inter-dependent and adjust their roles to best accomplish the children's bilingual learning. Their goal is two-fold: their children's educational success, and the linguistic survival of their family and community.

Negotiating roles as teachers and learners
Children themselves play an active part in each literacy eco-system. In any setting, the contribution of both children and adults to the family enterprise is important. From her observations of different societies around the world, Barbara Rogoff concluded that 'children and their social partners, particularly their caregivers, are interdependent rather than independent' (1990: 193). However, children's input becomes particularly vital in a new country where it is they who have knowledge of English and experience of primary school literacy learning. This may

require some negotiation between children and adults over each person's role in supporting younger children's learning. David Barton notes that 'roles are not fixed and unchanging things which people slot into ... they are negotiated, accepted and sometimes challenged' (1994: 41).

In such settings, children may be teachers of younger siblings at some moments, and learners from older siblings or adults at others. Again, movement between roles happens for children in most families, but it is highlighted in this kind of bilingual situation. Rogoff describes the relationship between learner and teacher as 'apprenticeship'. Apprentices are 'active learners in a community of people who support, challenge and guide novices as they increasingly participate in skilled, valued sociocultural activity' (Rogoff, 1990: 39). Bilingual children will sometimes be apprentices to parents, grandparents or older siblings when learning about literacy, and they will also spend part of their time in a teaching role with younger siblings as their own apprentices.

When developing their role as teacher, children draw on their experience as apprentice, using strategies they have observed at primary school or community language school as well as with family members. Gregory (2001) discusses how siblings take this input and fine-tune it for younger brothers and sisters, and how both older and younger participants gain from the interaction. In our project, we found that older children used a range of formal and informal approaches to literacy teaching, adjusting to their siblings' needs.

Different families, different systems

As we visited the home of each family in our research project, we began to realise that there were many ways of supporting children's learning. In Selina's family, her mother conducted formal lessons around the kitchen table every evening, teaching Selina and her sister how to read and write in Chinese. Yet Ming's mother did not act as his Chinese teacher. Instead, he could ask any one of his older siblings for help with his work from Chinese Saturday school. For example, his sister Chan would watch Ming writing Chinese characters, pointing out the tiny adjustments he needed to make.

Each of these families had different resources for literacy teaching. Ming's mother had six children so had less time for doing individual activities with them. But there were considerable possibilities for older

siblings to help younger ones. Thus family size is one factor in organis-
ing support. Another is literacy knowledge. Ming's mother placed
greater confidence in her children's knowledge of Chinese writing,
recently gained from Saturday school, than in her own. With regard to
English, her children were also the experts, since Ming's mother spoke
little English. Ming's twelve-year-old brother sat with him to read the
storybooks he brought home from primary school, sometimes reading
the whole story first with Ming re-telling it afterwards, or listening to his
younger brother read and prompting him when he was unsure: 'I tell
him the whole word and what it means'.

Ming's mother took the role of orienting her children to learning. For
example, when I asked her if Ming could bring his Chinese books to
primary school on a particular day, she encouraged him to take res-
ponsibility for doing so. She told Ming to look at me directly as I made
the request, and explained that 'If he hears you say something, he'll do
it'. Sure enough, Ming remembered his books on the day we had
arranged.

By bringing up her children to be independent learners, and ensuring
that the older children acted as helpers to their younger siblings, Ming's
mother had created a flexible literacy teaching system which took care
of her family's needs. All Ming's older siblings had gone to college and
university, and Ming in his turn knew how to pay attention to his
teachers and was achieving well at primary school.

Selina's mother supplemented the teaching of Chinese at Saturday
school with lessons of her own. She knew both Cantonese and
Mandarin, and was keen to pass this knowledge on to her children,
particularly since only Cantonese was taught in the community
language school. Selina's ten-year-old sister Susannah complemented
her mother's teaching by helping Selina to practise the Chinese characters that would feature in the following Saturday's lesson. Susannah's
methods were more informal than her mother's. Selina was allowed to
use colourful felt-tip pen instead of pencil, even though this meant
mistakes could not be rubbed out. Figure 42 shows a page from the girls'
work together. Susannah has demonstrated the characters first, and
Selina has then written the stroke sequence for each character in a horizontal row, using a heart symbol to cover up her mistakes.

Susannah also helped Selina with writing activities in English. The girls
made their own pop magazines and greetings cards, or played games

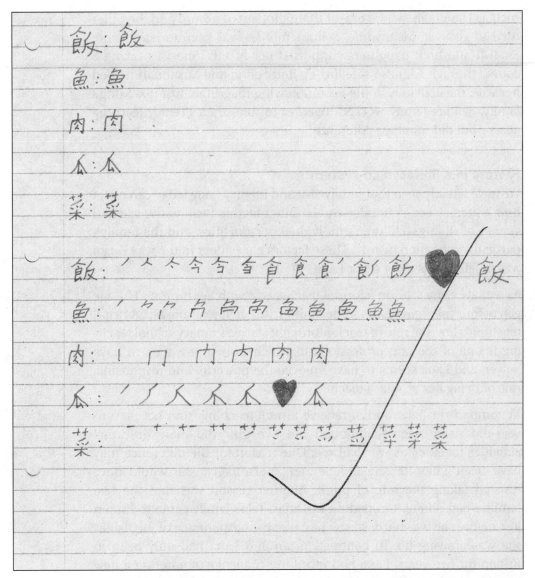

Figure 42: Selina working with her sister Susannah practising the sequence to build up Chinese characters. She uses a heart to cover up her mistakes.

such as Hangman, where one of them thought of a word and the other tried to guess it. Meanwhile, Selina's mother was keen to learn more English and both daughters supported her in this. She was taking a course through Chinese satellite TV and Selina and Susannah helped her with the activities in the accompanying magazine. Just like Ming's family, Selina's family worked together to fulfil their literacy learning goals – but did so rather differently.

Factors in a literacy eco-system

We have already seen that family size and literacy knowledge can affect how a literacy eco-system operates. Other factors include the age and gender of siblings, children's individual personalities, and the family's particular migration history. These factors are evident in the way Yazan was taught by his older sister Lana.

As we saw, Lana took on a formal teacher role with her brother. The age gap of four years gave Lana some authority in their relationship. As a girl teaching a boy, the role of teacher brought status. Primary school teaching is one of the rare professions in which women are seen to have power, and Lana seems to have enjoyed the powerful and responsible role of being her brother's teacher.

In comparison, Tala did not receive formal teaching from her eleven-year-old sister Nagam, although the two girls did many informal activities together, as we shall see. One reason for the difference may have been Tala's fiercely independent personality; she would have resisted taking the role of pupil. Another reason was that the two families had different migration histories. Tala's family came to Britain just before she was born, so she had plenty of experience of English as she was growing up. In contrast, Yazan and Lana had only been in Britain for two years. Lana had faced the challenge of entering a new language and culture at primary school, and wanted to support her brother now that he was doing so too.

The factors of family size, gender, age, personality, literacy knowledge and migration history are interlinked in their influence on literacy teaching roles, as shown in Figure 43. In each family, there will be a different interplay between these factors, which will result in a distinctive literacy eco-system. The system is dynamic and can change over time. For example, as Yazan grew more independent, Lana mentioned that their formal teaching sessions happened less often.

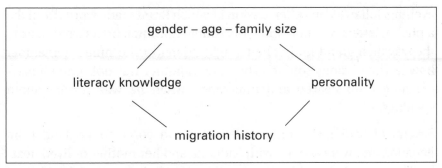

Figure 43: Influences on literacy teaching roles.

Extended family support

Brian and Sadhana were fortunate in having other relatives living with them or nearby – in Brian's case his grandmother, and in Sadhana's her aunts and uncles – who could also help them with literacy learning. These family members were part of the literacy eco-systems around Brian and Sadhana, playing their part according to their expertise in Spanish or in English.

Brian's grandmother helped him to spell words in Spanish, pointing out the need to put an accent in 'papá' (dad) and stressing the second vowel to show how the accent 'makes the sound hard'. She encouraged him to practise joining consonants and vowels to make syllables, just as he did at Saturday school. When she prompted him by asking (in Spanish) 'the M with the A, the M with the A – what does it say?', Brian responded with 'mamá'. He used cardboard alphabet letters to build up the word and this time he added the accent himself.

Next Brian assembled the letters for 'niño' (boy), reminded by his grand-mother to use the Spanish 'i' to give the correct sound to the word. As he moved on to 'niña' (girl), she asked him which vowel came at the end of the word and he replied 'a'. She then emphasised the typical gender endings in Spanish, saying 'niño es masculino, niña es femenina' (boy is masculine, girl is feminine). Brian showed his understanding by saying 'papá es un niño, mamá es una niña' (dad is a boy, mum is a girl), thus making conceptual links between all four words he had produced so far.

During this activity, Brian's eight-year-old brother Julian was sitting next to him and passing him the alphabet letters he requested. Sometimes Julian had his own ideas about which letter was appropriate, and his grandmother confirmed or corrected these suggestions. Later that evening, Julian led another session in which Brian made words from the alphabet letters. When helping his younger brother, he referred back to the way their grandmother had taught Brian to write 'niña': 'Remember how la Tita (Granny) did it?' Their grandmother was observing Julian's teaching from nearby and intervened when he was unsure about spellings.

Several of Sadhana's aunts and uncles had come to England from Ecuador, and were staying with Sadhana and her mother or lived nearby. They provided an additional resource for Sadhana's development of Spanish and exchanged knowledge with Sadhana about English, since they were learning the language themselves. Once, for example, Sadhana was writing a party invitation in English and asked her mother and aunt how to spell 'birthday'. To check the spelling, they decided to consult the large Spanish-English dictionary kept on hand for reference. Sadhana sat between the two adults, the three heads close together as they searched for the required page and found the entry for 'birthday'. Shortly afterwards, Sadhana showed me how to use the dictionary, turning the pages and pointing out a particular word.

Joint activity with adults – parents, grandparents, aunts and uncles – clearly stimulated the children's literacy learning. It also gave opportunities for older siblings to observe teaching in action, helping them develop knowledge and strategies as they themselves assumed a teaching role.

Different languages, different roles

In a bilingual family, the literacy eco-system may operate differently for English and for their home language, depending on the expertise of each family member. We can see such different balances in Tala's family. Her mother and older siblings, Nagam (aged eleven) and Khalid (aged

	mother	sister Nagam (11)	brother Khalid (8)	Tala (6)
English	Helps with writing and reading	Helps with reading, plays language games	Helps with reading, writes with Tala in play	'An independent learner'
Arabic	Helps with homework	Keeps an eye on homework	Less confident than Tala	'Tala just learns'

Figure 44: Literacy teaching roles in English and Arabic in Tala's family.

eight), played particular roles in Tala's learning of English and of Arabic, as Figure 44 shows. Tala's father was an important presence in her life but was often out at work when we visited, so we were not able to observe him helping Tala. To give a fuller picture, the table would have to be extended to include his contribution.

Nagam and Khalid took a prominent part in supporting Tala's English literacy learning, drawing on their experiences at primary school. Nagam read stories with Tala at bedtime, and found ways of helping her sister through informal activities such as language games: 'If I say a word, Tala can think of a rhyme'. She saw Tala as 'an independent learner', but gave invaluable back-up as a subtle and supportive teacher. Khalid also helped Tala to read in English, and I heard her ask him how to write words she found difficult when they were making greetings cards together. In many English literacy events, the three children were self-sufficient, relying particularly on Nagam's expertise. However, their mother was also fluent in English and helped Tala read the storybooks she brought home from school. She bought books on maths and English from a bookshop and used these in work with all three children for an hour a day.

With regard to Arabic, Tala's mother came to the fore as literacy teacher. She taught at the children's Arabic Saturday school and helped them with their Arabic homework on Friday nights. Nagam nevertheless made an important contribution, complementing her mother's teaching role. Although she believed that 'Tala just learns', she watched over this learning. If Tala started from the left-hand side of the page in her Arabic school exercise book, Nagam would remind her to begin from the right. When Tala was singing a song in Arabic for me, Nagam sat just behind her and quietly prompted her whenever she faltered. And Khalid's role in Arabic was quite unlike his dominant role in English. In many ways, Tala was more confident about Arabic writing than her brother, so he did not take the lead.

These changes in role were highlighted when the three children wrote a café menu together, first in English and then in Arabic (see Figures 45 and 46). This activity arose from a game they had been playing in their living-room, pretending to run a café. I video-recorded the event and present excerpts here from the transcript. The children could write their English menu without adult help, but needed support from their mother to produce the menu in Arabic.

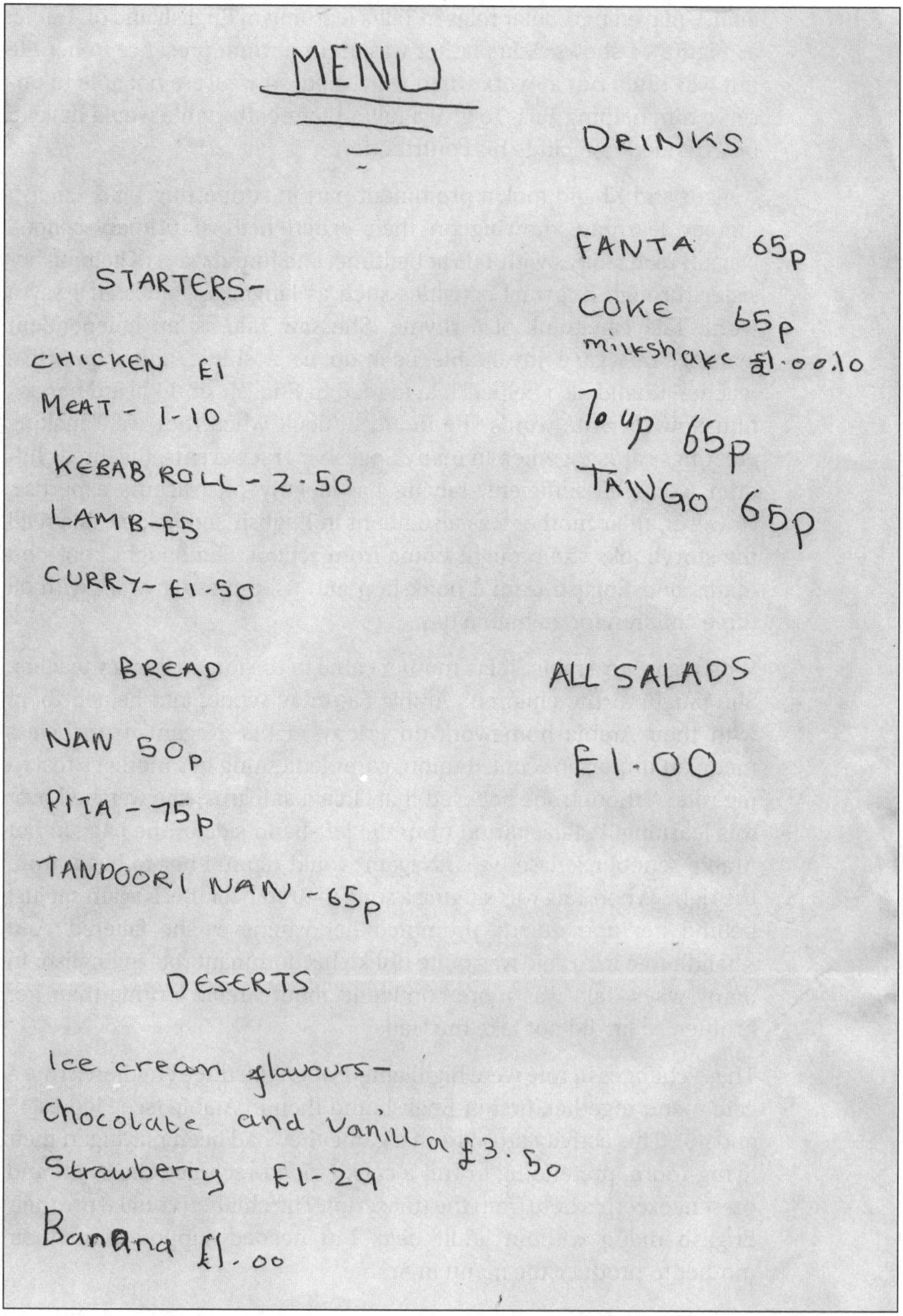

MENU

STARTERS-

CHICKEN   £1
MEAT - 1-10
KEBAB ROLL - 2.50
LAMB-£5
CURRY- £1.50

BREAD

NAN 50p
PITA - 75p
TANDOORI NAN - 65p

DESERTS

Ice cream flavours-
Chocolate and Vanilla £3.50
Strawberry £1-29
Banana £1.00

DRINKS

FANTA   65p
COKE   65p
milkshake £1.00.10
7o up 65p
TANGO 65p

ALL SALADS

£1.00

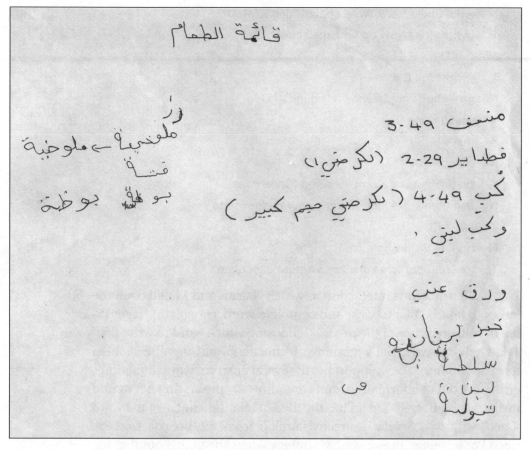

opposite: *Figure 45: Café menu in English written by Tala with her sister Nagam and brother Khalid.*

above: *Figure 46: Café menu in Arabic begun by Nagam and continued by Tala with her mother's help.*

Writing a café menu in English

Nagam, Khalid and Tala are sitting at the living-room table with pen and paper. Their mother is sitting on the sofa on the other side of the room, talking to another adult. When it comes to writing the dessert section of the café menu, the children decide to offer several flavours of icecream in their café. This extract from the transcript shows the moment when Tala begins writing with her older siblings' support.

N = Nagam (aged 11), K = Khalid (aged 8), T = Tala (aged 6)

T   (taking pen and paper from N) how do you spell vanilla?

K   V

N   write under here, write choco – chocolate

T   (writes 'ch') how do you spell chocolate?

N   C-H-O

T   (writes 'o') C-K?

N   no – choc (emphasises /k/ sound) – O

T   yeah I done O

K   that's H, S-H

N   choco – C-O

K   pretend you're – erm – writing 'Coco Pops'

N   and then write 'late' – know how to spell 'late'?

T   L-A-T-E

N   right (T writes 'late')

T   (reading out what she has written) chocolate

This is a harmonious interaction in which Nagam and Khalid combine forces to enable Tala to write the complete word 'chocolate'. Nagam is the overall organiser of the process, choosing which word to write first. Tala knows to write the beginning of 'chocolate', but then needs help from her siblings. They support her in several different ways, sometimes giving her direct information, and sometimes by prompting her to find the letters for herself. Khalid has the idea of relating 'choco' to the word 'Coco', with which Tala is already familiar from the breakfast cereal, Coco Pops. Nagam uses a similar strategy when she points out that the last part of 'chocolate' is the same as the word 'late', and Tala does indeed know how to spell this word.

Writing a café menu in Arabic

When they have finished their English menu, the children go on to produce one in Arabic. They become animated as they talk about their favourite foods, pointing out pictures of them on a menu from a local take-away restaurant. Nagam begins by confidently writing several items in Arabic. When it comes to Tala's turn, her mother starts offering suggestions from the other side of the room, and Tala then moves over to the sofa to get further support from her mother. Khalid's involvement changes significantly. He can no longer offer help as he did in the English event, but he quickly finds an alternative role.

N= Nagam, K=Khalid, T=Tala, M=mother, C=Charmian (videoing the event)
Arabic is transliterated and presented in italics
The English translation appears below

M *Tala bta'rfi tiktibi khubz Tala*
   Tala you know how to write 'bread' Tala

T *khubz ba'rif*
   bread I know

M *khubz...khubz lubnani*
   bread...Lebanese bread

T (trying to take the pen from N) mama mama

C don't fight don't fight – let's see, ask Nagam

N she can write *khubz*

C ah OK

K (to the camera) now she is writing 'bread' in Arabic

T (writes) *khubz* – is it '*kha*'?

M *kha* – *khubz lubnani*
   '*kha*' – Lebanese bread

T *heik?* (raising the paper to check with her mother)
   like this?

M *mish shaifi ana – farjiha – ruhi jibiha*
   I can't see – show me – come and bring it

T *heik?* (bringing her paper over to her mother)
   like this?

M *ah – huttin nuqat – en nuqat*
   yeah – put the dots – the dots

K (to the camera) she's going to her mum because she doesn't know
   how to spell 'bread'

Tala's mother is her main teacher of Arabic, and can therefore suggest a word she knows Tala will be able to write. Nagam agrees with her mother's idea that Tala should write '*khubz*' (bread). When Tala begins writing, she checks whether the word begins with the letter '*kha*', and her mother confirms that it does. Tala is still unsure whether she has written the letter correctly and goes across the room so that her mother can see. Her mother then reminds her to add the dots to differentiate the similar-looking letters.

Khalid is following the structure of the teaching event and understands the general issues involved in writing Arabic. For example, he knows that dots are important in Arabic script; shortly after this, he comments that 'my mum is saying – the dots...on the letters'. But he cannot give detailed advice to Tala about producing words in Arabic, so he decides to become the TV presenter of the Arabic event for an English audience (being aware that the video will later be shown to other members of the research team). Khalid's need to find a new part to play highlights the way in which roles shift as the language changes from English to Arabic.

Although the main role of teacher has shifted from Nagam to her mother, Nagam remains involved in supporting Tala's Arabic writing. When Tala moves across the room, Nagam comes to sit next to her mother on the sofa and leans towards the others to make sure she is still part of the interaction. She then begins to spell out the letters which make up the second word Tala is going to write, 'lubnani' (Lebanese). A discussion follows with her mother about which letters are needed.

N = Nagam, T = Tala, M = mother

N   *la ba nun nun alif* (Arabic letter names)

M   *aywa hiyyi bta'rif*

    yes she knows

T   (writing *lubnaa*)

M   *aywa lubnaa, aywa alif*

    yes *lubnaa*, yes *alif*

T   *nun?*

M   *aywa alif*

    yes *alif*

N   no no not *alif*

M   *lubnaa – alif taweele aywa*

    lubnaa – long *alif* – yes

When Nagam gives the letter names to spell '*lubnani*', her mother indicates that Tala might not need this help by saying 'yes she knows'. Nagam then questions the use of the letter '*alif*' and her mother explains that it is a different form, 'long *alif*'. Nagam has to adapt from taking a leading role in helping Tala with English to having only a supporting role in Arabic, but she accepts her mother's responses. She is also able to observe her mother's technique for teaching Tala, which involves prompting rather than giving direct instruction, and this seems to have influenced Nagam's approach to teaching her sister in English. Her apprenticeship to her mother in Arabic literacy teaching thus informs her methodology as Tala's English teacher.

Children's choice of teaching strategies

The older siblings in our research project proved sensitive teachers of their younger brothers and sisters. Their close relationship within the family had developed through playing and working together every day. The older children were aware of the younger ones' current literacy knowledge in each language, and the amount of information they could easily take in. This familiarity enabled them to choose strategies that worked well for each literacy event.

A lesson conducted by Lana with Yazan and video-recorded for the research project showed the range of strategies used: *demonstrating and testing, prompting, consolidating*, and *evaluating*. Lana first gave Yazan a spelling test in English, and then in Arabic, adapting the strategies to her brother's level of knowledge in each language. Figure 47 shows Yazan's answers to the test, and these are discussed below.

When the lesson was about to begin, Yazan asked Lana to do 'something easy for me in Arabic – not English'. He was emphasising that he had less knowledge of Arabic than English. This difference arose from the greater amount of input which Yazan received in English (five days a week at primary school) compared with Arabic (one morning a week at Saturday school). Lana was aware of this disparity and planned her teaching accordingly.

The English spelling test

Lana began with English, the language in which Yazan was stronger. Having reminded her pupil that 'today is the second of June' and written the date on the board, she began dictating words for Yazan – sitting on the carpet in front of her – to write on his sheet of paper. Announcing 'number one' in the test, Lana started to say the word 'school', but only got as far as 'schoo...' before she realised it would be rather challenging for Yazan. So she changed to an easier word, 'at', which Yazan wrote quickly and confidently. Lana followed this with 'no' and 'on' – apparently simple words but requiring Yazan to use the same letters in a different order.

Figure 47: Yazan's answers to the spelling test conducted by Lana in English and Arabic. He received a sticker for his efforts.

Item number four in the test was 'dog', to which Yazan responded with enjoyment 'doggie doggie'. Numbers five and six were 'cat' and 'bat', which he sounded out and wrote more slowly. Number seven was 'one', a slightly harder word to spell, but still familiar to him. So far he had written every word correctly. Lana was building up from two-letter to three-letter words, linked by theme (dog and cat) or by their spelling (cat and bat).

At this point she returned to 'school', but before giving Yazan the word she told him 'this might be a hard one'. Her comment signalled the greater difficulty of the word, that would require extra concentration, and reassured him that she would understand if he was uncertain about it. Yazan asked 'S-C?' but Lana felt that he could attempt it by himself, so answered 'just write it'. Yazan's version was 'skool'.

The last two items in the test were also more challenging: 'home' and 'look'. For 'home', Yazan produced 'hoym'. He hesitated on 'look' and Lana decided to give him a clue. She indicated that it was a long vowel sound by saying "look' not 'lock'." However, Yazan wrote 'loc'.

The test was now at an end and Lana announced 'I'm going to mark it'. Taking Yazan's paper, she ticked the words that were right and marked those where he had made a mistake with a cross. She gave him a model for the future by writing on the board the correct versions of 'school', 'home' and 'look'.

Lana did not find it necessary to use the strategy of *demonstrating and testing* (providing a model and then asking the child to reproduce it) for the words she gave Yazan in English. Instead, she first chose items he could easily write alone – to build his confidence – and then items which she judged as just above his level of competence, so that he could try to write them unaided. To help him with 'look', she used the strategy of *prompting*, by sounding out the word and emphasising the long vowel. She then marked his work, *evaluating* his spelling, and provided the right answers for words he had written wrongly, thus *consolidating* his knowledge.

The Arabic spelling test

When it came to the Arabic test, Lana acted rather differently. She began by asking Yazan to write '*arnab*' (rabbit), a word she had often taught him and hoped he would be able to write independently. However, Yazan demurred, though he was able to write the first letter, and asked Lana for help. She tried *prompting* him by sounding out the word, emphasising each phoneme, but he was still unsure. Lana quickly changed her strategy and switched to *demonstrating* the word on the board, writing four others below it to make a list of five. She knew that each of these words ('*asad*' – lion, '*baba*' – dad, '*mama*' – mum, and '*ax*' – brother) was familiar to Yazan from his lessons at Arabic school.

Lana was very careful about the way she demonstrated each word. Rather than writing rapidly as she usually would, she used a teaching technique she had observed at Arabic school – writing more slowly and making sure that each letter within the word was clearly visible, with the joins between them. For the letters which included dots, she put in each dot as she wrote each letter, instead of adding all the dots when she had finished the whole word. Speaking to Yazan in Arabic throughout the activity, she urged him to focus on what she was doing, saying 'stay with me'. Using Lana's model, Yazan wrote the word '*arnab*' on his sheet of paper, showing each letter clearly as his sister had done. Lana reminded him to add one of the dots.

She then gave Yazan a new challenge: 'Now let us see how we write *arnab*'. Yazan sat up excitedly. Whereas in English it would be a simple matter to read out the letters which constitute a written word, in Arabic things are more complicated because each letter has three different forms depending on its position in the word. Lana was asking Yazan to analyse this word by recognising the different letter forms involved – a common activity in Arabic Saturday school lessons.

Yazan named the letters which made up 'arnab': 'alif, rah, ba, nun' . Lana corrected the order of the last two: 'nun, ba' , and Yazan repeated her correction. Then she put a tick next to 'arnab' on the board, *evaluating* his response. He continued to say the names of the letters in the following words, with Lana *prompting* him where necessary by whispering the sounds made by the letters or tracing over the letter on the board.

One word, 'baba', caused Yazan particular difficulty and Lana noticed this. She shook her head and helped him to get it right, but commented 'you need more practice of that' and only gave him half a tick on the board. When he had spelled out all five words on the list, she said 'now tell me how we write baba again'. Lana was *consolidating* her brother's knowledge through making sure that he repeated the task, and this time Yazan did it correctly.

Lana gave Yazan a mark, *evaluating* his work by writing the Arabic numbers for 'five out of five' on the board. She told him to write all the words on the list by himself, setting a realistic time-limit for the task – he had twenty minutes to complete it – and promising him a sticker for doing it correctly (the same reward his teacher would offer him in Arabic school). As Yazan wrote, Lana continued to motivate him by saying 'quickly, carry on, you've only got fifteen minutes' and 'can everyone please hurry up – don't look at the board like you were watching TV'.

As Yazan approached the end of the task, Lana encouraged him: 'OK Yazan you're doing well, you've only got one more and we'll see if you get a sticker'. Having checked his work, and decided to be lenient about 'baba', which was still not quite correct, she offered him a choice from her sticker collection. Yazan wanted a Lego sticker, but Lana persuaded him to take a flower sticker, which she considered more appropriate ('let's get a happy one'). Finally, she negotiated with him about where to put the sticker – on his shirt or on his book – and when Yazan chose the latter, she placed the sticker in the middle of the page, between the English and Arabic spelling tests.

To deliver this bilingual lesson, Lana clearly drew on the teaching she had observed at primary school and Arabic school. She involved Yazan as an active participant, giving him just the right amount of support to accomplish each task. In order to do so, she brought different strategies into play at different moments in the event.

Guiding and shadowing

Two other strategies used by older siblings caught our attention during the research. As with Lana's teaching discussed above, these were fine-tuned to the needs of each pupil. At a time when Ming needed direct help with writing, his older sister Vicky used the strategy of *guiding* his hand. And at a moment when Tala needed only the slightest support to succeed in singing a song, her sister Nagam was *shadowing* her performance. These strategies can be clearly observed.

Because Chinese characters have to be written very precisely to be correct and not confused with similar ones, young children need to develop pen control at an early age. One way of doing this is to experience the feel of writing the different strokes through the hand movements of a more experienced writer. The child is learning kinaesthetically, via the sense of touch.

Vicky demonstrated the strategy of *guiding* through touch while helping Ming to practise Chinese characters one evening. She began by watching him write and making verbal comments, such as reminding him that it should be done 'nice and neatly, yeah?' As he did a horizontal stroke, she encouraged him to do it 'right across' so that it would be the right length. Then she started to move her finger across the page just alongside the stroke he was currently writing, indicating the length and angle that was required. She combined this action with comments: 'you've got to write like that' or 'go that way, down the middle, from that side...' She was leaning over to see clearly what Ming was doing, concentrating on the detail of his writing. At moments when he was finding it hard to translate into action her finger movements and verbal instructions, she put her own hand over his and guided his writing so that he could fully understand. Afterwards, Vicky remarked to me 'there's a particular way you have to write it'.

Although the strategy of guiding a child's hand is rarely used in English primary school teaching, partly because it is considered too directive, Vicky's support for Ming shows that there are times when it can be very useful. An older sibling or adult with whom the child feels safe and comfortable can offer guidance of this kind, which is particularly helpful when finding out how to do a physical activity such as handwriting.

Finally, the strategy of *shadowing* was demonstrated by Tala's sister Nagam, who saw Tala as 'an independent learner' who 'just learns' from the experiences available to her. Tala certainly displayed great determination, and preferred to go about things in her own way. Her older sister, however, was just behind her as she took each step – ready to catch her if she started to fall. This subtle support could be observed when Tala was reciting a poem or singing a song in Arabic, activities she loved. Nagam sat just behind her, closely following the performance and quietly voicing a word if she faltered, so that Tala could use her input immediately and continue without any apparent mistake.

Whereas shadowing is a hands-off approach to teaching, guiding is very much hands-on. The sensitive tutoring work of Nagam and Vicky shows us that each approach has its own usefulness, depending on the task involved and the needs of the learner.

Understanding literacy eco-systems

Like all families whose children are starting out in the educational system, bilingual families are keen for their children to succeed. Each family is likely to be drawing on the help of adults and older children to achieve this. If teachers can find out about the roles played by different family members and the strategies used, the school will be able to link in with each eco-system in order to further enrich the child's learning. The combination of home and school support will be a powerful boost to bilingual children's educational achievement.

Ideas for working with families

■ Find out about each bilingual child's literacy eco-system by asking parents or older siblings 'Who helps the child at home and with what activities?' Put together a fuller picture of children's all-round learning by taking account of literacy events in different languages. This information will help in deciding who to contact so as to support a particular aspect of children's literacy development.

■ Show that you value the different ways in which family members are contributing to a child's learning. For example, a parent may speak little English but may be ensuring that their child has space and time to learn at home. They may also be giving their child an orientation towards learning by encouraging them to pay attention to teachers' input and develop skills such as concentration. Make clear your appreciation of the work done by the family to help children learn the home language as well as English. When parents, grandparents or older siblings teach children about reading and writing, the skills developed transfer between literacies.

■ Link in with the vital role of older siblings as literacy teachers. Several schools have run successful projects in which siblings are encouraged to use particular strategies to support younger children's reading at home. You could make this an information exchange in which you also learn about the strategies that siblings already use. There may be some approaches the school has not thought of, or strategies particularly suited to siblings.

■ You could run a workshop in which children exchange ideas about how they teach younger siblings. Some children might be prepared to be videorecorded at home by another family member and the video could then be shown to the group for discussion. The aim of such work would not be to take over or re-shape children's approaches, but rather to encourage and support their expertise. Older siblings will benefit from knowing that their hard work is recognised by the school.

■ Families newly arrived in the country may need to build up their literacy networks and find mediators to help them as they get established. Many schools are aware of the importance of community support, and put families in touch with others who speak their language. The names and contact details of local community language schools can be shown on a prominent noticeboard, so that other families can find out about them. Local authorities should have information about community language schools, and the Resource Centre for Supplementary and Mother-Tongue Schools has an online directory of schools around the country on www.resourceunit.com. This helps families to make useful contacts and will contribute to the effectiveness of their literacy eco-systems, enabling children to maintain and develop their bilingualism and biliteracy.

Conclusion

Children who are becoming biliterate show us their capacities to learn in ways that we might not have thought possible. At the age of six, Ming and Selina understood that Chinese characters were made up of stroke patterns which held different meanings, and that English writing was based on the alphabet. Sadhana and Brian knew that alphabet letters which looked the same might sound different in Spanish or English. Yazan and Tala could switch easily from writing in Arabic to writing in English, changing directionality as they did so.

To people living in bilingual or multilingual societies, none of this comes as a surprise. In many countries it is considered normal for children to become literate in more than one language. For example, all children in Luxembourg learn to write in French and German as well as Luxemburgish when they begin primary school. In India, young children learn three languages: Hindi, English and a regional or local language, each of which uses a different script.

But to those of us brought up with only one language, research on biliteracy opens our eyes to the multiple possibilities for children's learning. It may seem strange at first that young children learning Chinese, for example, can write such complex patterns so accurately. A primary school teacher who looked through Selina's Chinese school exercise book was astonished by the characters she had produced at age five, and asked me 'How are Chinese children able to do this? Is it genetic?' I explained that I had observed the hours of careful practice put in by children at Chinese school, guided by their teachers. Any child whose learning environment emphasised precision in writing would develop the skill of pen control and the ability to analyse visual detail such as length and angle of each stroke.

Every society has particular expectations of children as they are growing up. We train children to fulfil these expectations, and assume that the training suits their capacities. Only when we gain insight into another society do we realise that our aims are culturally specific. Young children are capable of learning a great many different things. Their minds and bodies are flexible and they are eager to investigate whatever comes to hand. Often we place limits on them by deciding in advance what is or is not possible for them to learn.

This is why children's all-round learning, in homes and communities as well as at school, is so important. The different experiences gained in each setting complement each other, giving greater access to knowledge. Using the term 'complementary schools' to describe community language schools underlines this interweaving of support for children's learning in literacy and other cultural activities. The Chinese school offered Selina and Ming opportunities to try out calligraphy or Chinese chess, whilst also introducing them to a writing system which challenges the mind to work in very different ways from English. Tala and Yazan helped to present material about their families' countries of origin at the festival organised by their Arabic school; meanwhile, in class they learned to analyse the different forms of letters found in Arabic words. Brian and Sadhana could practise to perform in a play at Spanish school, as well as doing activities that reinforced their capacities to write alphabet letters or understand the concept of left and right.

We also saw the variety of ways in which support for learning was provided in the children's families. Some were formal: Lana using the little whiteboard in her bedroom to teach Yazan; Brian's grandmother helping him to practise the masculine and feminine endings in Spanish words. Others were less so: Sadhana sitting beside her mother and aunt as they searched for words in the Spanish-English dictionary; Ming and his brother writing and drawing together on the computer; Selina and her sister making their own pop magazines; Tala producing a café menu with the help of Khalid and Nagam. Each family used a mixture of formal and informal approaches, drawing on the resources of different family members.

All the children were at the same time learning in primary school, where the curriculum was focused on a single language and literacy, and on certain targets to be achieved. In comparison to the overall richness of their lives and learning, this curriculum was relatively narrow. The children's variety of experience at home and in their communities was an important complement. The primary school teachers who became involved in the project were keen to find out what happened at home and community language school, and were fascinated by what they discovered.

Primary schools can respond to the diversity of children's learning experiences in two key ways. Firstly, schools can consider how to provide a more diverse curriculum which enables children to explore a wider content and develop a greater range of capacities. The chance to learn different languages at primary school is one example. This benefits both bilingual and monolingual children – and community languages need to be included. Literacies which involve different scripts and different directionalities will heighten children's visual and actional capacities as well as giving them access to new cultural worlds.

Secondly, schools can give recognition to the work done by families and communities in contributing to children's learning. The staff at community language schools need remuneration, resources and training. This is an issue for central and local government to address, but schools can assist by offering premises and sharing resources and training opportunities. Community language teachers are dedicated to helping children grow up bilingual. They deserve our support.

Families are at the heart of children's learning and we need to acknowledge and appreciate their contribution. Early years educators can make suggestions for collaboration, taking account of each family's unique combination of resources and relationships. By working in harmony with the variety of learning experiences in young children's lives, teachers can play a vital part in each child's development as a bilingual and bicultural individual.